THE   INTUITIVE   TAROT

VIDEO and AUDIO TAPES by Richard Gordon

How to Read the Tarot Cards (video)

Spiritual Light Journey (audio)

Journey to the Golden Pyramid: A Guided Meditation (audio)

Crystal Contemplation (video)

How to Pray and Meditate (video)

THE INTUITIVE TAROT

A METAPHYSICAL APPROACH TO
READING THE TAROT CARDS

BY

RICHARD GORDON

WITH

DIXIE TAYLOR

FOREWORD BY

Amy Zerner and Monte Farber,
Artist and Author of *The Enchanted Tarot*

Blue Dolphin Publishing
1994

Published by Blue Dolphin Publishing, Inc.
P.O. Box 8, Nevada City, CA 95959
Orders: 1-800-643-0765
Web: www.bluedolphinpublishing.com

ISBN: 0-931892-84-8

Illustrations from the Universal Waite Tarot deck reproduced by permission of U.S. Games Systems, Inc., Stamford, CT 06902 USA. Copyright © 1991 by U.S. Games Systems, Inc. Further reproduction prohibited.

Library of Congress Cataloging-in-Publication Data

Gordon, Richard, 1955–
    The intuitive tarot : a metaphysical approach to reading the tarot cards / by Richard Gordon, with Dixie Taylor ; foreword by Amy Zerner and Monte Farber.
        p.   cm.
    Includes biliographical references.
    ISBN: 0-931892-84-8 : $13.00
    1. Tarot. 2. Spiritual life. I. Taylor, Dixie, 1957– .
II. Title.
BF1879.T2G647 1994
133.3'2424—dc20   94-10403
                                                    CIP

Cover design: Richard Gordon

Printed in the United States of America

10   9   8   7   6   5   4

This book is dedicated to
Thomas-John Grieves,
the man who set my feet
on the path of Tarot.

TABLE OF CONTENTS

FOREWORD

Intuition is what truly guides us to and through all of our positive life experiences and even to the transformative understanding that can come from the apparently negative ones. In our own lives we have found the Tarot to be a tool that enables us to develop this divine ability—all we need add is our sincere desire to grow and our open hearts and minds.

In *The Intuitive Tarot,* Richard Gordon shares with us his understanding and respect for these special gifts. Through simple explanations and exercises, he helps us to connect with our Higher Selves and offers gentle insights into experiences encountered when reading Tarot cards, either for yourself or for others. This book presents universal truths and timeless metaphysical wisdom that we can never be reminded of too often. The importance of meditation and preparation for readings is discussed, along with that of the ritual and sacred art of the tarot.

With clarity and love, the authors emphasize spiritual balance and teach us how powerful our intuition is when we nurture and trust it. It quickly becomes apparent that the answers to our every question lie within ourselves.

The Intuitive Tarot is like a conversation with a trusted spiritual mentor. How fortunate that we all can now interact with such a loving guide, a friendly voice with a unique ability to make timeless wisdom accessible and enjoyable.

—Amy Zerner and Monte Farber,
artist and author of *The Enchanted Tarot*

PREFACE

This book is based on a series of lectures given by Richard Gordon during the spring of 1989, and a video cassette on Tarot entitled *How To Read the Tarot Cards: A Metaphysical Approach.*

Richard began his adult life as an engineer. After he was introduced to the Tarot cards, he listened to two audio cassettes and started reading the cards himself. Within a year, he was reading professionally. One year after that, he produced the Tarot video cassette. Shortly thereafter, even though readings flowed naturally, he began to feel guilty about being paid for something which came so easily and in which he had little formal training. In response, he bought some books on Tarot and borrowed a few more. As he began to read, a wave of confusion overcame him. No two books viewed the same card in the same way. The words of a teacher rang in his ears, "The answers are not in a book—they are within you." Guided by that inner wisdom, he put the books back on the shelf and never picked them up again.

Richard Gordon travels extensively, both nationally and internationally, presenting lectures and workshops in the areas of self- and spiritual development, in addition to providing individual counseling. His video cassettes, *How to Read the Tarot Cards: A Metaphysical Approach, How to Pray and Meditate, Crystal Contemplation,* and the guided meditation audio cassettes entitled *Spiritual Light Journey* and *Journey To The Golden Pyramid—A Guided Meditation* are distributed internationally. The Tarot video has made national best-seller lists.

Richard's purpose in all of his work is to help people better understand themselves and live from their own higher wisdom, through spiritual enlightenment and personal empowerment. You may find that Richard's approach, grounded as it is in solid metaphysical concepts, brings a clarity to your understanding of the Tarot cards that is lacking in other books available on the market.

This book is not intended to provide all of the answers but to assist you in your own search and to suggest some areas of focus. Look at this book as another tool to assist you in your own search for the truth. Ask questions. Maintain a healthy skepticism. And above all, trust yourself and your own higher wisdom. You will be able to recognize truth when you find it, wherever you find it. We hope you enjoy reading this book as much as we enjoyed writing it.

—Dixie Taylor

THE INTUITIVE TAROT

1

INTRODUCTION

When a child is born, he is born with the genetic pattern for becoming a whole adult—a Co-creator with his parents, lacking only experience. Made in the likeness and after the image of God, we are primarily spiritual beings of light and love, just as God is. Lacking an awareness of our essential spiritual nature, we exist to gain the experience necessary to get in touch with who we are and always were. The entire purpose of our existence is to unfold to a total experience of ourselves and our at-one-ment (or attunement) with God. During our earth walk, opportunities are naturally presented for us to gain this experience. When "awake," we seize these opportunities and grow from our experiences. Our awareness is the key in experiencing Oneness and unfolding to a fuller recognition of our true selves.

Our job as teachers is to help you empower yourself and to facilitate the process by which you teach yourself and reach conclusions—in effect, acting as a catalyst. As readers, our job is to help you to learn more about yourself, assist you in getting in touch with patterns which you are activating, and to help you to see the effects of the patterns. We can then provide recommendations on how to change unproductive patterns and their effects, or reinforce productive patterns.

Sometimes the beliefs and perceptions that people hold of themselves get in the way of their full enjoyment of life, in ways that they cannot see initially. All the good in the world is here, and it always has been here. You either perceive it, or you don't, but that doesn't change the fact that it is here. Take, for example, a question of worthiness: a person who holds an essential belief in his lack of worthiness may find that this erroneous belief affects him in his relationships, his work, his monetary situations—everything. The longer the belief is held, the stronger the pattern becomes and the more negative his life experience is. But when that person can see the effect of that pattern and chooses a more productive direction in life, then he has taken the first step in reasserting control of his life. This step is the result of awareness through honest self-analysis.

Often, only after understanding the cause/effect relationship of the unproductive belief pattern can a more balanced pattern be chosen. The new pattern provides a point of focus which allows the energy of attention to flow through the balanced pattern, not out of the unbalanced one. With time, the person sees his environment reflecting more of his new beliefs and less of his old ones.

To recognize a more balanced pattern, it is important to ask three questions: Who am I? Why am I here? (Or what is my purpose here?) Where am I going? These three questions must be answered in order. The answers to these questions will come as a result of meditation, contemplation, or some other form of personal quiet time. As we get a handle on the answers, focus develops in life. All other questions or apparent problems can be referenced back to this information to obtain a balanced perspective. Direction in life begins to appear. This direction provides a focus for your mind, emotions, and actions. Balanced patterns begin to appear and unbalanced ones begin to dissolve from lack of use.

As you walk the path of self-development, any patterns standing between you and your growth will surface to be dealt with. Rather than fighting an unbalanced pattern (or kicking yourself because it is there), focus attention upon what you do want (the new pattern). It is up to you whether you create from your desires or your fears, loves or hates. With time, the universe will give you what you place your energy into. Since energy follows thought, as a man thinketh in his heart, so it is. Anything can be created with persistence, patience, and love.

Working with the Tarot cards helps you to identify patterns and their possible consequences. They can also help you answer the three big questions and replace non-productive patterns with productive ones. You can also get a sense of how likely an outcome is and how long it may take to appear. Before we answer these questions and talk about the cards, there are a few other things to discuss. Hang in there, we'll get to the cards! When we do, you may find that the other material which we have covered may be more valuable to you personally, and as a reader, than the work that we will actually do with the cards.

Always remember:

TRUTH AND ALL OF YOUR ANSWERS ARE WITHIN *YOU*—
NOT THE CARDS!
THE CARDS MERELY PROVIDE A POINT OF FOCUS
THAT ASSISTS YOU IN ACCESSING INNER TRUTH!!!

2

METAPHYSICS DEFINED

Metaphysics is defined as the study of things which are not physical, or beyond the physical. It is, in a thimble, the conflict between science and religion. Five hundred years ago, what is today called "science" was known as "metaphysics" because it could not be measured or studied in an empirical method by using the tools available at the time.

Metaphysics is also a belief, a knowing to the point of certainty that we and the universe are more than just our physical bodies. It is a recognition that we are also spirit, soul, and energy, and as such are governed by certain unvarying rules. Perhaps the scientists, studying ever smaller and smaller bits will someday come close enough to reach out and touch the face of God—and on that day, the saying goes, they will find that religion has been there all along (Quote from *Reader's Digest,* July-September 1989, quoting from the movie, *CREATOR*).

There is nothing mystical about the study of metaphysics. Neither is it new. It has been around for thousands of years, its concepts scattered throughout a thousand religions. Metaphysics can be nothing more complex than the study of the fundamental laws of the universe and how they affect life. But it can also be the study of ourselves, each other, the world, the universe, the face of God and the piece of God which rests within each of us, as well as the study of the energy behind the physical manifestations. Come, and learn. . .

3

THE MIND/BRAIN CONNECTION

The mind and the brain are not the same thing. The mind is more non-physical than physical. The brain itself is a tool of the mind. While the mind works with the whole of the body—in particular the central nervous system, the brain, and the spinal cord—the brain is separate and different from the mind itself.

Let's talk about brain waves for a second. The frequency for Delta is 0-4 cycles per second—also known as hertz. For Theta, 4-8 cycles per second, for Alpha, 8-13 cycles per second, and for Beta, 14-26 cycles per second. During our waking periods, the brain wave frequency most often encountered is Beta. When the brain waves are in Beta, we are primarily operating out of the left brain, the analytical side. When the brain is functioning in the fast Beta frequency, it is difficult for us to get in touch with the higher levels of the mind—the subconscious and superconscious levels. By working with deep breathing, muscular relaxation techniques, visualizations and other meditative techniques, we help to quiet the mind and still the body. When this occurs, the brain wave pattern begins to slow down. It begins to shift from Beta to Alpha. As this occurs, the conscious mind slows to the point that it can begin to become aware of what is happening in the higher levels of the mind—the subconscious and the super-conscious levels. The conscious mind is now able to attune itself to receive greater levels of intuition, psychic ability, and spiritual experience. You could also say that as the brain waves slow down, the left brain starts becoming more receptive to the right brain. The left brain is thus associated with the conscious mind, and the right brain is associated with the subconscious mind.

Not coincidentally, the frequency of nature is Alpha: that's why, if we are agitated, it frequently helps for us to go for a walk in the woods. We have a tendency to harmonize with our surroundings. So a person who is agitated and operating in Beta, by walking in nature tends to start moving in Alpha.

As a person becomes more relaxed, the brain wave pattern moves into Theta. The problem with this is that Theta is normally a sleep-cycle pattern. Most people are not able to go into Theta with conscious awareness. They tend to either go to sleep, or to lose conscious awareness as to what is happening. Disciplined yogis are able to go into a Theta brain wave pattern, and retain conscious awareness. Some yogis are also able to go into Delta with awareness. Needless to say, if people have trouble staying awake in Theta, they definitely have trouble staying awake in Delta.

When most people are reading, they are going to relax into Alpha. At this point they can become attuned to higher levels of the mind, the subconscious and superconscious, and still retain conscious awareness. At this point there is a good balance between left brain and right brain. You don't necessarily have to be in Theta or Delta to access information from the higher mind. In Alpha, the person is able to bring through images, impressions and feelings, and still maintain conscious awareness. If you are reading for yourself or someone else, obviously it is important to maintain enough conscious awareness so that you can communicate what you are picking up. That requires a good bridge, or a good connection between the conscious and subconscious mind. For most people, this is best done by going into Alpha. As I mentioned earlier, there are some rare individuals who can go into the even more restful brain wave cycles, Delta and Theta. At these levels, it may be possible to get in touch with even higher levels of awareness, but there is really very little research indicating what happens to a person when they are in Theta or Delta.

While reading, you need not be concerned about which brain wave pattern you're operating from. Simply relax your body and do some breathing exercises to still and center your mind. Upon experiencing relaxation, start the reading. Do some rhythmic, deep breathing if you become tense during a reading. We will discuss preparation for a reading, including relaxation methods, in the chapter on Meditation.

Now, let's explore how we use these three levels of mind.

4

DIVISIONS OF THE MIND

The brain can be divided by hemispheres—the left brain governing logical and rational aspects, and the right brain governing intuitive and creative aspects. The mind can also be divided into levels—conscious, subconscious and superconscious.

Picture a pyramid, divided into three sections going up. The bottom level or base of the pyramid is the conscious mind. This level of the mind works primarily with the left brain. The next level up, sitting right on top of the conscious mind, is the subconscious mind. This level of the mind works primarily with the right brain. The level at the top of the pyramid is the superconscious mind. Each division of the mind has different functions.

CONSCIOUS MIND. The conscious mind tends to be more masculine and its strengths are logic, reasoning, analysis, and structure. It works in the here and now, using the information gathered from the five senses. It is limited by space and time, and the accuracy of the data at hand.

The conscious mind cannot directly access information which may be in the future or the past, or which is outside the range of the senses. Additionally, any conclusion which the conscious mind reaches is subject to being inaccurate, due to the inaccessibility or incorrectness of any vital piece of data. Inaccuracies can also result from a person expecting or wanting another conclusion.

10

The language of the conscious mind is verbal. Most people operate from this level almost exclusively. While in a Beta state, the conscious mind is usually unreceptive to the higher levels of mind.

When the body is relaxed or in "reverie," a state experienced immediately prior to falling asleep or immediately upon waking up, the brain waves shift from the more rapid, daytime Beta waves into the Alpha state. Meditation, hypnosis, daydreaming, and some forms of brainstorming also cause this shift in brain activity. At these times, we begin to allow the awareness from our superconscious and subconscious to filter, or trickle, into our conscious awareness.

SUBCONSCIOUS MIND. The subconscious mind tends to be more feminine, and its strengths are intuition, creativity, the abstract, and dreams. The subconscious mind is not limited by space or time, but has access to the lines of probability into the future, as well as events from the past. It is able to tune in regardless of physical distance, and thus transcends the limitations of space. The language of the subconscious mind is primarily pictorial.

The subconscious is the storehouse of all your experiences, past knowledge, understandings, and patterns—those from your past incarnations as well as those in your present one. These patterns are both balanced (productive) and unbalanced (unproductive). It is the subconscious mind's responsibility to create what the conscious mind places its attention upon. The clearer the picture (focus) and the stronger the feeling (emotion), the more easily the idea is received. Since the subconscious does not judge "good" from "bad," it is thus our challenge and responsibility to maintain a conscious awareness of where our attention rests, or what it rests upon.

The subconscious is the part of your mind that remains when the conscious mind is sloughed off with each physical death. The subconscious mind contains the reasons you chose to come into life as you are, why you chose this body and these circumstances.

Today, an integration process is occurring. During this time period, we are allowing men to become more intuitive, and women to become more analytical so that individuals as a whole are now more balanced. As we develop an ease in working harmoniously with both brain hemispheres, and the conscious and subconscious minds, a door opens to receiving insight from the superconscious.

SUPERCONSCIOUS MIND. The superconscious mind is the most difficult to access. It is the part of the mind which is in contact with God. Within it resides your God-Self. To access this level requires consistent inner attunement. Some of the great masters have been able to access this level, as well as to operate from it.

The superconscious mind, with its connections to God, is like a seed which contains the blueprint for awareness of who we are, our development, and our purpose. As seeds propagate according to kind, so through evolution do we unfold to a full expression of this perfect pattern. We have and always have had the full potential—we only lack an experience of it. Life provides opportunities for this experience.

On the subconscious and superconscious levels, we are all interconnected. The subconscious mind can be compared to a computer terminal. The superconscious mind is the main frame, or the master bank that your terminal is networked into. The programmer, representing the conscious mind, is the person accessing the subconscious. Remember always that a smart programmer can tie into the mainframe and access more information than that stored on the discs at your terminal. When truth is coming from the subconscious or super-conscious levels, Richard will refer to that as guidance from the Higher Self. The Higher Self is in contact with the Universal or Collective Mind along with the Akashic Records, the storehouse of all wisdom and knowledge in the universe.

In working with the Tarot cards, you are stilling the conscious mind so that it is receptive to insights from the Higher Self. There are several challenges the conscious mind likes to create. First, it likes to maintain control and thus is reluctant to allow higher awareness to come through. The second problem is related: the conscious mind likes proof, and unfortunately, by the time an intuition can be confirmed, it is frequently too late to act on it or to take advantage of its insights. Finally, it tends to rationalize everything, the result being that the conscious mind sometimes plays tricks. This rationalization, the rearrangement of truth to fit a preconceived notion, can even go to the point of denying what has been experienced, such as accessing the Higher Self in meditation. It is sometimes better just to experience first; it takes the conscious mind's preconceptions out of the process until later. In seminars, Richard prefers to allow the participants to experience the higher levels of the mind in a guided meditation first. After the experience, the conscious mind has a much harder time saying that it is impossible.

The higher levels of the mind often communicate with pictures, such as those encountered when sleep closes down the conscious mind. The information which you receive in dreams comes from the subconscious and the superconscious minds; however, because the subconscious is not limited by space, time, or distance, you can perceive what has happened not only in the past, but events which have occurred in past lives. Additionally, you can perceive lines of probability for the future and connect with God or other people.

You are not taught to use your intuition in school, only logic. But to reach the top in any field which you choose, you must be able to draw on both logic and intuition. This is the "marriage made in heaven." The term is a symbolic reference, which implies a marriage within, combining and balancing both the male and female forces, the conscious and intuitive processes.

5

HOW THE MIND MANIFESTS

Holy Wisdom maketh all men free from fear,
Wide of heart, and easy of conscience.
Holy Wisdom, the understanding that unfolds forever,
Continually, without end,
And is acquired through the holy scrolls. . .
—The Angel of Wisdom, *The Gospel of the Essenes,* p. 162

If being able to do anything, go anywhere, and have virtually anything we want is why we come here and choose to exist on this plane, then why do the children of rich parents have the highest suicide rate? Why are the privileged, who have the freedom and the means to do almost anything, unhappy enough to try everything until they kill themselves? They are living their lives backwards. The key is in the order that things are accomplished.

1. beingness
2. doingness
3. havingness

Life must be lived in this order—first concentrating on the quality of being within yourself, then on the expression of this being by doing, and finally by reaping the rewards of the doing which springs from being by having. This is working from the inside out. "Seek ye first the kingdom of God (within yourself), and all these things shall be added unto you" (Matthew 6:33). You must get in touch with yourself first, and you do this through meditation, contemplation, and inner attunement. We will have more on meditation later.

The laws of the universe control "manifesting," or rather, your ability to manifest the things that you want, desire or think about. The subconscious mind, which is responsible for controlling manifestations, does not judge good or evil. It only sees and creates, responding to the demands, desires and fears of the conscious mind. The higher mind works in pictures. So if the conscious mind can picture something clearly and put energy behind it, the subconscious mind will manifest it, be it "good" or "bad." By not being in touch with yourself, with your essential beingness, and by not being aware of the things upon which your thoughts rest, you may be inadvertently and blindly using the laws of manifestation to create the very things that you fear.

Why is that? Two reasons—thought and emotion. Anger and fear are extremely strong emotions, and thus we can all picture and feel *very clearly* the things we fear, so therefore we do a better job of manifesting what we fear. The clearer the picture, and the stronger the emotion, the better the reception.

However, you can learn from any situation—everything contains an opportunity! "There is never a problem without a gift for you in its hands" (*Illusions: Adventures of a Reluctant Messiah* by Richard Bach). If you are interested in learning more about the mechanics of manifestation, may we suggest that you investigate the really excellent series of books by Sanaya Roman, especially *Creating Money, The 4-T Prosperity Program* by Stretton Smith, Shakti Gawain's book, *Creative Visualization* and Napoleon Hill's book, *Think and Grow Rich*.

What concerns us here, and what the cards can help us to recognize in others and ourselves, are patterns. If you think a thought often enough, you create a pattern which may be brought through in this life, or later. Your life experience today is a result of all past and present thoughts and beliefs.

The thoughts in your mind are more important than you have heretofore realized. Think of it this way: if the thought is energy, then the energy may affect matter, since matter is just a denser form of energy.

Energy = Matter. For hundreds of years, Newton's Principles reigned supreme, and people believed that energy was something that you *did* to matter. So it appears. Most of what we have on the physical level is too heavy to be moved very much or very far by the use of thought. But that is only true on *one* plane. It is not true on others. The physical plane is only the plane of results. What you think about has an impact on the physical plane, however, since it becomes real on this level. The thought, which starts at the upper level, slows down as it comes down into the denser energy levels of the physical plane. Remember, the thing is and always has been energy. It is just energy at a different resonance level.

The physical body is important because it is the vehicle we have chosen for this lifetime. It is, in effect, a mirror which allows us to see what we are manifesting on another level. You can find the same type of mirror in relationships. Or in your jobs. Or in the presence or absence of financial abundance. This physical plane is our playground, our fertile ground of creativity. It provides a tangible expression of our spiritual, mental, and emotional selves.

The keys are the pictures and the emotions. Your subconscious mind has the duty to manifest whatever the conscious mind puts its attention upon. Subliminal messages and affirmations are rough ways to activate the laws of manifestation by the use of patterns. If you are going to be working with this type of patterning, be sure that you know what the messages are. If the message is, "I don't want to be *fat*," realize that the picture being sent is *fat*. You may be working against yourself. So be careful where you put your attention. Always use affirmations which emphasize the positive. Action follows thought, and the energy flows where the attention goes.

Your conscious and subconscious will be in the closest connection right before you fall asleep, and right as you begin to awaken. If you do your affirmations at these times, the messages, and more importantly, the pictures and energy, go into the subconscious more easily.

Patterns of thought do create in the physical plane. One of the dangers of fixation, or of psychoanalysis is that reexperiencing can become reliving, and re-energizing. By continually harping on a thought process, or searching out causative factors or fixing blame, you are re-creating an event and giving energy to it.

You are not capable of divided attention; you can only put your attention on one thing at a time. Even though your thoughts may oscillate between two or several thoughts in quick succession, you only deal with one at a time. There are some positive ramifications to this: if you are energizing what you *want,* you can't be energizing what you fear.

Some thoughts come unbidden, but you don't have to let your mind dwell on them. If a fear comes up, don't beat yourself over the head because it is there—that not only creates dis-ease, but also re-energizes the thought. Simply remove you attention from it, and bring your attention back to what you want.

Every thought that you allow your mind to touch goes into your subconscious, which has contact with the whole world. So watch your thoughts when you are injesting anything—the news, the fight at the dinner table, even the meal. The *meal?* Certainly, the preparer of food lays over the food at the time of preparation the thoughts and emotions which he is experiencing in his own mind. So when you inject the food, you also inject his energy. How about Joe the chef or cook, who had a fight with his wife before he came to work? He starts reliving the emotions in his mind as he prepares your food—thinking how angry he is at her. He gives the food to you, and you eat it. You have just injested all of that emotional garbage—and suddenly you find yourself really angry at your wife!

There is an old adage that food prepared with love tastes better. Think about it. But since you can't always be certain, it is better to bless your food, and cleanse it before you eat it. Send light and love into it, so that it may better tend to the needs of your body, or so that it tastes better.

You can use the laws of manifestation to create more than you are aware; visualization and manifestation need not be made difficult. Why put hurdles on the universe? Why demand that a thing be manifested to you in such and such a way and no other? To satisfy your curiosity? If it comes to you from unexpected sources, it still comes, does it not? Why not just accept it? Focus on your desire and allow the universe to provide.

On the subconscious level, there are no boundaries between people. A kind thought that you have may be received by one or more strangers in diverse parts of the world. Their uplifted experience may result in thoughts, words, or actions which benefit one or many.

How does manifestation tie in with reading the Tarot cards? Through the importance of programming—for you and for the person for whom you are reading. What are you looking for? What are they looking for? How is your subconscious to know what information to retrieve? Program yourself on the conscious level to bring through the information which the person wishes to work with and is prepared to work with. Program yourself also with the sure knowledge that the reading is done in alignment with the greatest and highest good for all concerned.

To create wisely, you should get in touch with the God-Self, so that you may receive insights from it into what is best for you. Then, you develop your goals. Next, put your attention upon the goals, and send them out into the universe with joy. Now, wait expectantly for this energy to cycle back. When it comes, be prepared, and take action on the opportunities. Finally, give thanks for all your blessings.

Notice that in this pattern, you are either acting or being receptive. This is the masculine/feminine cycle of creation. Masculine, feminine, masculine, feminine, etc., in alternating patterns. This is the pattern of the universe. To be a full creator, you must use the active and receptive energies together in balance. This pattern is also the cycle of giving and receiving.

6

DEALING WITH PATTERNS

All things were created to assist in growth or survival—and to help you learn. The operative word here is "learn." That which does not assist in growth or learning any longer must either be changed, or be pruned back and set aside, like unproductive limbs on a tree.

The patterns that you are currently operating from may have come from previous lifetimes, or they may have been created in this lifetime to assist you—by yourself, or by your parents. As children, we were told many things during the growing process.

The initial patterning given to us by our parents was intended to provide an external structure for us to work within. It helped us to learn to control ourselves, our environment and our emotions. The world, without a structure for comparison, was and is full of random factors. Thus, we depended on our parents, initially, for guidance.

Children come into this realm with a conscious mind which is like a blank slate, operating primarily from an intuitive level, and soaking up everything like a sponge. Children operate from a level of truth and light and love, watching and observing. They observe and learn from everyone in their environment. They accept what is told to them as truth. This allows them to be imprinted with certain behavior modifications and "to do's."

Unfortunately, however, the following scenario sometimes takes place: data, in disgruntled little pieces, is entered into our computer brain—*garbage in*—"Mom/Dad/Someone said, "Don't trust anyone; you're so stupid; you're so clumsy; you're so bad/good; you always spill your milk when you pour it." The subconscious mind only stores this stuff. The conscious mind, however, manipulates the data, and files it into "Like Files," putting all of the data that seems to match, even remotely, into the same file, where it seems to pile up. All of that garbage by itself has no power. However, as the data collects, the child begins to draw conclusions which develop into beliefs. As the beliefs grow in strength, so does the energy behind them. The child cycles it over and over and over again in his mind, until it manifests into reality, and becomes a self-fulfilling prophesy—*garbage out.* The child's belief, that "I always spill my milk when I pour it," may have ballooned into the adult's belief that "I am a failure." He thinks about it over and over and over again, putting energy into that thought pattern. Then when he creates tangible results in his environment, he points at it, and says, "There's the proof!" Congratulations! You have successfully used the laws of manifestation! However, you have used these laws against yourself.

The "to do" patterns given to the child by his parents are not intended for his detriment. They are passed on so that the child may successfully negotiate the obstacles which he might encounter—either societal or environmental. As we outgrow the need for such patterns, we can then exercise our freedom to change them. We can learn to operate from a higher level.

When you learn to operate from a higher level, you also learn to take responsibility for the factors in your life. You chose to come to this physical level, to experience the lessons which are here to be experienced. You chose your parents, both because of what they could teach you, as well as what gifts you could bring to them. And you have chosen to experience life from the perspective you are currently experiencing, whether or not you are currently in touch with the specifics of those choices. Again, the operative word is "learn." We have all come to learn. Even now, you are holding this book in your hands because of your desire to learn. As an adult you have an opportunity to look at your life patterns and choose to replace those which have outlived their usefulness—regardless of whether they were ever useful or not. Working with the Tarot can help you identify and evaluate your patterns.

Everyone has major patterns at play in their lives. For most people, these patterns are productive; however, one or two of them may cause significant challenges (I don't like the word, "problems"). A major pattern will affect *all* the areas of life—relationships, finances, health, and career.

How can a single pattern affect so many areas? The conscious mind tells the subconscious what to do. A thought will therefore activate a corresponding subconscious pattern, and effects will flow from that interaction. This energy is expressed each time the person thinks the same thought. Resultant effects of this process are seen in all areas of his or her life, and the person gets mired down in the results.

Often, at this point, they blame anyone and everyone else, and send out a picture to the universe that everything is conspiring to screw them over. Then they focus their attention and energy on just how they are being screwed over. This is dangerous, because the subconscious and the universe are not there to make value judgments on whether the picture being sent for manifestation is good for you or not. Once again, like the computer maxim—GIGO—garbage in, garbage out.

When you send trashy thoughts in, you will manifest trash back out. You are using the laws of the universe to create garbage for yourself. In this example the person is in the process of creating or reinforcing unproductive conscious and subconscious patterns. Repetition of this cycle produces even more unpleasant effects which strengthen the person's belief that caused the initial problem.

The *key* is to go in and release the pattern. If you are stuck in the physical, you are stuck in the effects. Thoughts are things. You must go back to the causal level—to the thoughts. Ask yourself, what is the person thinking about, what are they feeling, what emotions come up? If one or two of these attitudes can be corrected, or rather, called to the attention of the person so that *they* can correct them, then many of the things out of balance in their lives will fall into place. They must go back to the point of cause—the initial thought—and ask, "What do I want to create?" "What do I want now?" *As they change their beliefs and thought patterns, they are literally changing their future.*

The reader's job is to tune in on this level and see the process that occurs. You choose how your environment affects you. This choice is made in every situation, either consciously or unconsciously, depending on whether the conscious mind is on auto-pilot. Don't buy into the cop-outs. Think about this: if it was done *to* you, then you can do nothing. Poor victim. But if you have *put* yourself there, then you can pull yourself back out of the situation. And this puts the power back into *your* hands.

Now is the beginning of the rest of your life. Choose never to access that garbage file again. Choose to access the *I am worthy* file. Let the garbage file start to collect dust. When you are accessing a new pattern, and reinforcing it, things that are not in harmony with it will begin not only to collect dust, but also to decay, and with time, to disappear. Because the contrary file is no longer being used, it is no longer compatible with your new, higher vision of yourself. You are reprogramming yourself at a higher level. This energy pattern is one that you can carry with you into your newly created future and express it with every thought, word, and action.

If this is so, then why do bad things happen to good people? Consider, the "happy face" may be merely a façade— a smile does not mean that the person inside feels in harmony with his outward appearance; some of the most jovial people are also some of the most angry. But they refuse to express or deal with the anger and hostility, turning it instead inside, where it attacks the body. The concept of a loving God does not harmonize with a picture of God sending bad things down to us. But the idea of *us* creating it does make sense, if we created the situation because we needed to learn from it and work with it. Secondly, we may be reaping the results of thoughts, words, and actions preceding this lifetime. Some people call this *karma*. Finally, a commitment to spiritual growth causes unproductive and limiting beliefs to surface. As we deal with these issues and move to a higher level of consciousness, unpleasant events may be experienced in our lives while releasing an old pattern.

To release a pattern, you must consciously choose another. There may initially be some resistance to a new pattern—so just work through it. What is important is not whether you are better or worse than someone else, but whether or not you are adding to yourself, from where you are. You don't earn the right to go on to the next lesson until you clean your plate on this one.

The sequoia tree grows to be three hundred feet tall and lives five hundred years—almost forever, from our perspective. The seed of the sequoia is very, very small, and about the width of a couple of sheets of paper. The size of the seed is not important—within it is the blueprint for its entire potential. The seed IS the adult, lacking experience.

One such seed became a bonsai tree. Like its counterpart, the bonsai is now several hundred years old. But unlike the sequoia who has reached upward for its full growth, the bonsai is only eleven inches tall. The bonsai came from the same type seed, had the same potential, but it has been manipulated and limited, and wired down. The bonsai has no control over what has been done to it—it has been truly limited by outside forces.

Even if we limit ourselves from our full potential as co-creators with our God, we still retain the blueprint for what we were destined to be. What would happen if the bonsai was planted in the ground, even now? That potential is still there within us—still available to us. And the good news is that if we have done it to ourselves, then we still have control over it. If we got ourselves into it, then we can still get ourselves out. If we have not done so already, it is time to plant ourselves in good earth, provide plenty of water, and remove the wires.

"When thine eye is single, thy whole body also is full of light" (Luke 11:34 King James translation). If we align the conscious and subconscious with the superconscious mind, then we will allow ourselves to be filled with light from the Creator. The superconscious is where your God-Self resides. If we ask for assistance, it will be there. The only relevant question is whether or not the information is valid. We need to draw from this level, yet still be grounded. We need to operate from the whole brain, without putting down the physical body which we have chosen.

Most of us will be operating from the subconscious when we tune in. A few persons have consistently operated from the superconscious mind, such as Jesus and Buddha. They went through this whole process, just as we do. Jesus said, "The works I do, so shall ye do, and greater works still" (John 14:12). He taught that "the kingdom of God is within you" (Luke 17:21) and advised his disciples to "enter into thy closet, and when thou hast shut thy door, pray to thy Father which is in secret" (Matthew 6:5). Here you find truth.

Having tools to find your own truth is self-empowering. That is what this book is about. Often, going to another to receive your answers results in giving *them* your power. This is why we stress the importance of trusting yourself, and your own intuitive flashes, in dealing with your own life and in reading the Tarot cards. When you read for another, keep this in mind. Pass on tools to them so that they do not become dependent upon you.

7

OPENING A CHANNEL
TO THE GOD-SELF

Prayer and meditation are flip sides of the same coin. Prayer is a message sent to God—an assertive process. In reality, everything we think is a prayer. Meditation is an expectant listening, a receptive process. In meditation you allow yourself to be receptive. *Do not set expectations about the fruits of meditation.* You may not get answers or flashes of insight. Instead, the payoff may be in being at the right place at the right time, setting productive events into motion (the benefits of which may not be seen until later), or in the flashes of insight which you receive during the day. Even more important than this will be the peace you experience and the loving harmony you express to the world! The purpose of meditation is to contact and live from your God-Self.

The God-Self is the small, still voice within. Zen Buddhists say that if you can describe it, you haven't got it. There is a lot of truth in that—you can't explain what the God-Self is. The more you try to explain it, the further you get from the truth. It has to be experienced. But in order to experience it, you have to get into a meditative space.

There are several ways to do this, but almost all of them start with the breath. Slowing down your breath slows down your heart, which slows down the processes of your body and the combustion reaction which occurs as your body is functioning. Then select a point of focus for your mind. It can be a master, a principle (such as light or love), a *mantra*, your breath, a crystal, a card, or a spot on the wall—any point that you can bring your mind back to when it strays. The most productive focus will be one which causes you to experience a sense of upliftment and spirituality. Holding the focus and taking deep rhythmic breaths stills and centers the mind, calms the emotions, and relaxes the body. You begin to shut down the receptions from the five senses and begin bringing the energy of the body into the central nervous system—the brain and the spinal cord.

Through repeated meditation a strong link is built with your God-Self. The peace which you experience in meditation can then be carried into your daily activities. A calm balance is created in which you can more fully access higher levels of consciousness at will. When you choose to read Tarot cards, the peace and concentration developed during regular meditation will serve you well. It will help to slow you down to a point where you are receptive (an agitated mind is not a receptive mind). It is during this receptive state that the channel to the God-Self opens, allowing the intuitive flashes to drop down into your conscious mind.

The next chapter contains a guided meditation. You may want to read this guided meditation into a tape recorder, so that your mind is free to enjoy the experience. If you would rather, you will find an order form for this guided meditation at the end of the book.

8

GUIDED MEDITATION

You are about to embark on a relaxing, guided meditation. At the end of this meditation, you will be asked to close your eyes and experience whatever occurs while in this relaxed state. Feel free to remain in this space for as long as you wish. When you want to come back to your easy chair, simply recall the room as it was before you left—feel the physical sensations of the body; wiggle your fingers and toes; take a deep breath, and when you are ready, open your eyes. If you would like, you may record this meditation yourself on a cassette, or you may purchase a similar meditation from Richard, using the information at the back of this book.

Settle into a comfortable chair, with your back straight. Uncross your arms and legs, and relax.

Take a deep breath, inhaling to the count of seven. Hold your breath until the count of seven, and exhale to the count of seven.

Continue this wonderful, centering, and enlivening breathing process. Upon inhalation, feel relaxation coming

---

This guided meditation is also available on an audio cassette, entitled *Journey to the Golden Pyramid: A Guided Meditation*, combining the voice of Richard Gordon and the harp music of Gail Barber. *The Spiritual Light Journey* guided meditation audio cassette combines Richard Gordon's voice with Craig Evans' synthesized music. You may find these tapes beneficial in opening yourself to higher levels of awareness in preparation for using the Tarot cards. For your convenience, an order form is available for these tapes at the end of the book.

into your body. On exhalation, experience the release of all tensions, all worries, all concerns, whether they be spiritual, mental, emotional, or physical.

As you continue this wonderful breathing pattern, you are becoming more and more centered, more and more balanced, more and more in harmony with yourself.

Now, simply allow your breath to ebb and flow at will. See a beautiful white ball of light directly below the soles of your feet. Recognize this as Mother Nature, a very relaxing, calming source of energy. Allow this energy to come into the soles of your feet, and penetrate every cell there. Now allow this beautiful energy to flow up your ankles, past your knees, and into your thighs. Now every muscle, every tendon, every ligament becomes loose and limp—totally and completely relaxed.

Now allow this relaxing energy to flow up into the buttocks area, and into the abdominal area. Any tension here simply drifts away. Allow it to dissipate.

Experience the relaxing energy flowing up into your chest; now up into your shoulders, down into your upper arms, past your elbows, into the forearms, hands and fingers. Any tension in this area flows off the ends of your fingers, just like water flowing off the edge of a leaf.

Now feel the relaxing energy flowing up into the neck, up the back of the head, into the scalp, and down into the facial muscles. Experience this area loose and limp—totally and completely relaxed. Now experience the relaxing energy flowing into the brain.

If any tension remains, anywhere in your body, allow it to flow down through your body, down through the soles of your feet to the center of the earth, knowing that there it will be balanced and transformed into something of harmony.

Now see a beautiful white ball of energy directly above the crown of your head. Recognize this as the Father energy. Great light, great love. Recognize this as a connection with the universe, with God, with the High Self, or whatever aspect you recognize as being the greatest and highest good in the universe.

Allow this energy to flow in through your head, to localize in your heart area, and allow this light and love to expand throughout the whole of your body, and feel its energy mingling with the loving energy coming up through your feet. Allow this energy to flow throughout the whole of your body, and into your aura. Know that this source of energy is infinite, and always available—all you need do is ask for it, and it will be given. Recognize that you are totally and completely protected, in all dimensions, on all levels, in all spaces and times.

Now let's take a little trip. You are walking along the beach—it is a beautiful sunny day. You look up, and the sky is blue, and the warmth of the sun on your body feels so good! You hear the sound of the waves as they rush up on to the shore, and feel them ripple over your feet. The water feels so cool, so soothing. As you walk along the shore, you can feel the individual grains of sand caressing the soles of your feet.

Now, to one side, you see a path that leads into a forest. You take this path, and are amazed at the beautiful colors of the rainbow, in the sky, in the plants, in the animals, in the earth itself. You see violets, the indigos, the blues, the greens, the yellows and golds, the oranges and the reds, and you feel a part of it all.

Now you hear the gurgle of a brook to one side. You step off the path and into the water. The water is so clean, so clear. You can clearly see your feet. You walk up the brook a ways, see a waterfall, and step under it. You feel the water splashing over your body. Cup your hands and take a sip of this pure, clean water. You realize that you have been cleansed completely, within and without.

You step back onto the path, and now you hear a beautiful sound vibration in the distance. You look up and see a beautiful golden pyramid, and you know that this universal sound is coming from this universal space. You walk along and, as you get closer, see a beautiful, radiant being standing at the foot of the pyramid. You recognize that this is a guide, one who has complete insight into the secrets of the pyramid. As you walk up, this person takes you by the hand, and you feel completely comfortable. The door at the base of the pyramid slides open, and the two of you walk in. You feel very, very comfortable in this space, and know that inside this pyramid are the secrets of the universe. Anything that you desire at this time, and are prepared to work with, is available for you. If you wish additional guidance, simply ask for it, and know that it will be provided. You will remember everything that occurs, and bring it back with you. Now close you eyes and enjoy this personal time, and personal space—enjoy your adventure.

Each image in the visualization had a function. The white light coming in through the soles of your feet is the feminine energy. This sends a message to your body to relax, and begins to heal it. The white energy coming in through the crown of your head is a masculine energy, the God or universal energy. These two energies were mixed in the heart to bring you balance, a balance of the female and male, or *yin* and *yang*.

You sent any imbalances in energy through the soles of your feet into the center of the Earth, knowing that this unbalanced energy would be transmuted there into something of balance and harmony. You should always replace the energy you send out with something of light and love, so that you do not replace the imbalances you sent out with something else out of harmony. This replacement energy came in through the crown.

The individual at the base of the pyramid was an aspect of your Higher Self, a guide, teacher, guardian angel, or master. The pyramid itself represents a higher level of consciousness which includes the Akashic records—the storehouse of all the wisdom and knowledge in the universe. You acknowledged that you desired to access information for which you were ready and willing to work with. This is important, because there is no sense in accessing information that you're not ready to work with. At this point in the meditation you went into the pyramid. It is possible to access information on either a conscious or an unconscious level— and whether you remember it or not, you have brought back something which will help you access this information more easily in the future.

This guided meditation works with all of your five senses, and with the psychic senses associated with each. These psychic senses are as follows: seeing—clairvoyance (clear seeing), hearing—clairaudience (clear hearing), touching— clairsentience (clear feeling), tasting—clairgustation (clear tasting), and smelling—clairolfaction (clear smelling). Additionally, there is a sixth psychic sense, which is not associated with any of the physical senses: clear knowing. This is a knowing which is not the result of a logical process—rather, one second the information is not known, the next moment it is. Your experience of this meditation helps you be more receptive and accurate when you work with the Tarot cards.

This meditation, or one similar, is an important exercise for stilling and centering the mind, calming the emotions, and relaxing the body. Reaching this relaxed state allows you to slip easily into the state of mind which you will be using when you give a private consultation, in either reading for yourself or someone else.

9

WHY WORK WITH THE TAROT

I have reached the inner vision,
And through thy spirit in me
I have heard thy wondrous secret.
Through thy mystic insight
Thou hast caused a spring of knowledge
To well up within me,
A fountain of power, pouring forth living waters,
A flood of love and of all-embracing wisdom
Like the splendor of Eternal Light.
                    —The Angel of Eternal Life
             The Gospel of the Essenes, p. 166.

We are the seeds of the Creator. In meditation, we become aware of what always has been and what *is*. Growth is endless, and our potential is unlimited. More is possible than you are currently aware. As Jesus said, "Truly, truly, I say to you, He who believes in me shall do the works which I do; and even greater than these things he shall do. . ." (John 14:12-16 Lamsa translation from the original Aramaic).

Where are we supposed to learn these things that Jesus promised? "The Comforter, the Holy Spirit, whom my Father will send in my name will teach you everything, and remind you of everything which I tell you" (John 14:26).

"When the Spirit of truth is come, he will guide you into all the truth; for he will not speak from himself, but what he hears he will speak; and he will make known to you things which are to come in the future" (John 16:13-15).

This Holy Spirit, this God-Self who communicates with you, is and always has been present within you. As you go into deeper levels of meditation, the breath and vibrations of the body slow down even further. This opens up our awareness and perceptions, creating the silent place to hear the small, still voice within, known as the Higher Self.

The Tarot cards can be used as a point of focus. Working with pictures in the beginning of this process, while slowing down your thoughts along with your breathing, encourages this process to work, because pictures are often the language of the higher levels of the mind. The cards are a tool which can help you develop your ability to open the door to go into the higher levels of consciousness. By choosing to use that door, you will make the connection stronger.

Can you use this process *without* an outside focus? You *always* have a focus—focus on *that* spot on the wall, *that* point on your forehead—and you can go anywhere you want within; eyes open or eyes closed, it makes no difference to your altered state. We all have the ability to go within, without an external point of focus.

Our purpose in working with the Tarot cards is to use this point of focus to develop greater attunement with our own higher wisdom and, if we choose, to use this open doorway to help others. The Tarot is a great tool because the images, colors, astrology, and numerology can all be used in reading. As you practice, more insight into the cards, patterns, the working of thoughts, energy, and most importantly, yourself will develop. My hope is that many spiritual and psychic insights will come to you. You may perhaps be led to the point that additional use of the Tarot is unnecessary for receiving inner attunement and guidance.

10

READING: GOING WITH THE ENERGY FLOW

And truthfulness in Thought, Word and Deed
Will place the soul of the faithful man
In the endless light of Eternal Life
>   —The Angel of Eternal Life
>   *The Gospel of the Essenes,* p. 165.

No one knows where the Tarot cards came from, except that today's cards are similar to cards which were used in England five hundred years ago. The playing cards in use today are derived from the Tarot cards, lacking only the major arcana. Public attitudes towards the cards have ranged from ridicule to reverence.

Don't sanctify the cards. There is no magic in the cards. All the power is, and always has been, within you and the person who gives you permission to read for them. Do not give your power away to anything outside of yourself. Recognize that the cards are merely a tool, like a shovel. You can dig a hole in the ground with your hands, or you can use a shovel. Although using the shovel will save you a lot of time, the shovel itself on the ground does nothing—you must put your energy into it. The cards are like this—nothing without the reader. As a tool, the cards are useful in connecting you with your higher levels of mind, and in helping the person you read for to make the same connections. But these same connections can also be made without the cards—and that may be your goal.

This approach is metaphysically based to allow the enlightenment of the universe to come through. There are other mediums that allow the same flow of energy and information—dream analysis, palmistry, tea leaves, crystal meditations, etc. But they all hold in common one thing: they are channels to allow the Higher Self to come through.

There are a number of misconceptions about the Tarot cards—that they can only be used to predict the distant future, or that they are merely the tools of con-artists, fortune tellers, and misguided individuals. An even more serious misconception is that a Tarot reader can do no wrong. The cards are no better or worse than the person using them and their intentions.

In the hands of a spiritually minded person, the Tarot can unlock hidden talents or unravel lifelong problems. They can help tap into personal levels, which most people are unaware of. But the Tarot only reflects the self—and every reader is coming from their own perspective. We choose the level and quality of information revealed by the level of our growth and inner attunement. To best use the Tarot cards for our growth and spiritual development, we, or the reader we are going to, needs to be:

1. focused on spiritual development;
2. calm and well centered; and
3. asking that the most beneficial information come through in the most understandable form before even picking up the cards.

When you choose a Tarot deck, look for vivid pictures. There is a reason for this—pictures are the primary language of the mind, and the more vivid the pictures, the more the cards will trigger insights. *The Enchanted Tarot* by Amy Zerner and Monte Farber, artist and author, is a wonderful deck for people who love fantasy and fairy tales. The Rider-Waite deck contains a wealth of symbolism, as well as vivid imagery. The Hanson-Roberts deck has soft, loving colors and images. The

Universal Waite combines the best of the last two decks. For
that reason, we will be referring to the Universal Waite deck as
the cards are discussed in Chapter 13. If you are using a
different deck, some of your intuitive definitions for the
individual cards may vary. However, even using a different
deck, you will find that the same patterns appear in the layout,
even if different cards come up.

What you will be bringing across as you read depends on
where you have placed your attention. As you place your
attention on what you want, you activate not only the patterns
that are there, but also the powers of the universe. Likewise,
the more knowledge you have, the better understanding you
will have of the messages and symbolisms you will be dealing
with. The pictures on the Tarot cards are not derived from a
single doctrine, but from many, including numerology,
colorology, and astrology.

What you will be identifying in the reading will be the
patterns. Do not expect these patterns to be the same for every
person—everyone is unique. What is right for one may or may
not be good for everyone, or for anyone else. In some cases,
it may even be detrimental. Try to be as non-judgmental as you
can. The more neutral you can be about the results, the less
your conscious mind will distort the information.

Your attention, as either reader or seeker, determines
which patterns are activated. Everyone comes into life with
different strengths and weaknesses. A pattern may be im-
proved by adding new knowledge, or decreased in strength
and importance by not focusing energy there. Unfortunately,
some coloring is impossible to avoid. But as the reader, you
need to limit any urge to render advice which does not come
from your Higher Self. Trust that the channel which you open
up to your Higher Self will allow the right information to come
through in the right form. Ideally, this will come through
uncolored, but you must separate the wheat from the chaff
even in the best of readings. If the information coming through
does not ring true for the person seeking the reading, then it

should be discarded. But how do you separate the information that isn't correct from the information that you don't want to be correct? This is always a problem, so be guided by your inner self. As a reader, the information may not make a whole lot of sense to you; try to be clear, but don't filter it overly much as it might make perfect sense to the person receiving the reading.

The future is not set. Therefore, you cannot tell the future absolutely. We all have free will. Thus it may be that an aspect of a reading, although valid at the time of the reading, may not manifest at all. As a thing is in the process of manifesting, or moving from a higher level to a more dense one, you are always interacting with the subconscious mind. At any time, it is possible for you to alter the course of a manifestation.

But think about the alternative: if we could predict the future with complete accuracy, then that would mean that the future was already predetermined, that we had no free will, and that everything was set in stone at the moment we were born. If that were so, then there would be no reason for us to go through all of this. We *do* have the power to change our course, to change our future.

So what does that mean to you as a reader? Well, unfortunately, it means that you will be dealing by necessity with uncertainties. It means that the questioner may avoid the negatives and may also foul up the positives. Focus your attention on the probabilities and possibilities. What you will be looking for are the clues as to how close a thing is to manifesting. Look for how tangible, physical or clear the thing looks or feels; the clearer the vibration, the closer to manifestation that aspect is.

As a reader, you will want to
1. tune in on a spiritual level, opening up your intuition (use breathing and meditation techniques discussed in the preceding chapters),
2. get in touch with the patterns of the seeker,
3. look at the energy involved, and
4. see how things are manifesting.

All right, this next is very important: before you tune into another person, make sure that you protect, ground and center yourself. You do this by using a white light visualization:

Breathe in light and love. Breathe out your disharmony and dis-ease, sending it clothed in white light into the center of the earth. Replace your disharmony with something of harmony and balance, light and love. Picture light coming in through the crown of your head, and going out through your feet (grounding). Experience more energy coming through the crown and send it to the heart region (centering); and then allow that light to expand through your whole body and out to your aura. (For additional balancing you may be directed to bring energy from your feet into the heart region.) Know that you are totally and completely protected in all spaces, times, and dimensions via your God-Self and Beings of Light. Focus on a feeling of warmth in the heart area, allow yourself to feel open, and experience a flow between the head and heart regions.

This visualization doesn't take very long, but don't skip it. If you're going to be sensitive, you don't want to pick up another's garbage. If you do find yourself picking up garbage, which you will notice as tenseness in your body, a lack of clarity, or an attachment to what occurs in the reading, let this garbage flow out of your body—you don't need to hold it in yourself to help another. Feeling what they feel, sympathizing instead of empathizing, does not lessen their pain, nor does it help their growth, so let go. Let this garbage flow down through your feet, and allow the energy to come in through your head. If you close this channel off, because of fear, inattention, etc., then you will be using your own energy, and you will feel depleted at the end of the day, and possibly faster, depending on how quickly you allow yourself to be drained.

At the end of the reading, you will again need to cleanse and clear your energy field. Here you will be doing a series of three double inhalation / exhalations, and then a single inhalation / exhalation, using the following visualization:

Inhale twice through your nose in the same intake, seeing pure white energy coming in through the crown of your head. Exhale twice through your mouth in the next exhalation, seeing the energy going out through your feet. Repeat this same process two more times. Then make one final, deep, and slow inhalation. Fill yourself to completion with clear, clean, white energy for yourself and your energy field, and see the energy flowing outward and around you as you slowly exhale. Now send some of this beautiful, loving energy to Mother Earth. This helps to balance our planet.

Then go wash your face and hands. You are now ready for the next reading.

Pay attention to your energy level. This will become easier the more you work with it. This not only applies when you are working with the Tarot cards, but throughout your day. As you become more sensitive to the energy flow around and through you, you will know when you are blocking the energy; you will feel heavy, unenergetic, or tight in the stomach, shoulders, back, or head region. Energy is being sent to you all through the day, some balanced, some unbalanced. People who work with the public and feel drained at the end of the day have absorbed unbalanced energy which blocks the flow of spiritual energy into and out of themselves. Once they have used up their own energy, they need to be recharged.

Check your energy and be aware of its flow. Do you feel out of balance? If so, CLEAR, CHARGE, AND GROUND. Bring in as much spiritual energy as you can use—it doesn't run out; there is not a limited amount that you are allotted. As you learn to pull energy in from the universe through the crown of your head, and from the earth at your feet, you will feel more energized and grounded. Additionally, you won't unknowingly be pulling energy from anybody else. And if you are surrounded by white light, no one can pull your energy from you without your permission.

Work with the energy from the heart region. This is the center of universal love, as well as the balance point for the energy coming in from your head and your feet. As you allow yourself to feel a warmth in the heart area and feel open from the head to the heart, the information you receive will come from an accurate, loving source, be clearly perceived, and be given in an unconditional, non-judgmental fashion.

11

MORE ON READING

All [those] who are hungry [for the truth] upon the earth shall eat and worship before the Lord; . . . my soul is alive to him.

—Psalm 22:29, Lamsa translation from the original Aramaic

Before reading for yourself or others:

1. Use a breathing technique to still and center the mind, calm the emotions, and relax the body.
2. Perhaps do a meditation.
3. Allow energy to enter in through your crown, opening your spiritual channel.
4. Allow any out-of-balance energy to flow through your feet into the center of the earth for transformation.
5. Feel the universal, unlimited energy flowing through you. Allow it to expand into your auric space.
6. As you read, allow the energy to come in through your head and project it outward from your heart.

Visualize a pyramid behind the person for whom you are to read. Allow any of their unbalanced energy to flow through the pyramid and be transmuted into healing energy. See a bridge between that person's Higher Self and yours. Visualize people on the bridge whose job it is to monitor the energy, and to give to you what you need. Pray to be a clear vessel. Know that the most beneficial information will come through from the highest source and will deal with areas which they are prepared and willing to work with right now. Also, affirm that this information will come through in the most understandable fashion for them.

The seeker may be going through a very natural releasing process of energy. By throwing off energy, they can get down to other energy. If you prepare and hold the space open, they don't have to be concerned with what happens to the energy they throw off. And your space won't absorb the negative energy.

Not all of the information which will be sent to you will make sense, but realize that that is all right. Remember that this information is not for you, but for them. Allow the information to pass through to them without letting it affect you. Realize that they have created these situations for their own sake and learning. Don't take it into yourself.

You will get impressions in different ways—seeing, feeling, hearing, tasting, smelling, or knowing, or combinations thereof; however you perceive it is fine. Go with your first impression. But be aware that once you start processing the information, your conscious mind may kick in and cloud up the issue. You may also not have all of the picture before you need to start passing along the information. Take a risk. Trust and allow. Sometimes the second part of the information can't come through until you give the first part to the seeker.

Time is the most difficult factor to deal with. Look at the sense of energy. Look for a feeling of clarity or solidity—a brand new idea may appear as hazy, because the lines of probability are so distant. Other things will appear very solid. The subconscious and the superconscious don't deal with time—the past is now, the now is now, and the future is now. So look at the surroundings for clues to seasons. But is it this year, or next year? It is *very* tough to get a handle on this. Remember that you can *ask* "when." Go with your first impression, and then ask for clarification—three what? Days, months, or years?

The other problem you may run into is that the person may be working on a series of things—A to B to C. You may pick up information on C, even though they will have to deal with A and B first. How fast or how slow they will do so depends on how quickly they handle A and B. Depending upon the person and what they are dealing with, A and B could take two weeks, two years, or two lifetimes to complete.

All of the situations in which the seeker is involved have been created by them to learn. The process is ongoing, and it is important to enjoy the process along the way. It is also equally important to fully appreciate each step, and move on. Don't get so fixed on the future that you ignore today. All of this was created by you so that you could educate, improve, and perfect yourself.

When the information is coming through, you are in an altered state. If you begin analyzing the information, you will tend to block the flow. Instead, stay very relaxed—as relaxed as you are right after meditation or while in reverie, that period either right before or right after sleep. If you begin to feel nervous or out-of-center, pause and do some deep breathing. This will reestablish your spiritual connection.

It is a good idea to record your readings—both for yourself and for the seeker. They may not remember details in a reading anymore than you will, because particularly sensitive seekers will go to a higher state with you. When the conscious mind comes back down, the reading will fade away, just like dreams fade upon awaking. Recording the readings will also be useful to you by helping you to get time perspectives worked out a little bit better, and to check your own accuracy.

Often, people coming in are very nervous. They have fears, and may be afraid that you may access what they've kept secret. Because of this, their nervousness or fears may block the energy flow. You can only read what they will allow you to. Sometimes, no matter how good the reader is, the energies just don't mesh. Do your best to relax them, and yourself. If all avenues remain blocked, say so, and stop the reading. Don't make them wrong, but don't make yourself wrong either.

There may be times, even for an experienced reader, when a single word, or a single piece of information will be all that comes through. Try not to have preconceptions or expectations as to what the reading is going to look like, or how it will come out. Go with the energy flow. You may even feel like there is a block in the energy flow because not much information is coming through, only to find that you have given the most important piece of information, and given it in a way that is understandable for that individual. Perhaps the individual came for only that one piece of information.

There will be times, especially if you know the person very well, that you may just pick up things out of the air. But beware of giving unwanted advice. Often, unsolicited advice or comments are only resented. You have only two choices— asking if they want your perspective, and abiding by their answer, or saying nothing. There are times when it is better to say nothing. Each person proceeds at his or her own pace, and should not be rushed into awareness. Use your intuition— each situation will be different.

What about good news and bad news? Don't sugarcoat it, but realize that there are beneficial aspects in all things. Every situation is either a millstone or a milestone. Situations, in and of themselves, are neutral. Each of us determines, based upon our actions and attitudes, whether the situation is going to be beneficial or detrimental. *Every* event is an opportunity for growth!

If you perceive a person operating from an unbalanced pattern, and you can foresee some of the ramifications of this pattern, then you have an opportunity to look at the causes and see how that person is creating their situation. You can then talk with them about cause and effect relationships. If the client doesn't like the ramifications or the effects of that pattern, which of course is *their* decision to make, not yours, then you may give recommendations as to some things that they can do to help develop a new pattern which is more abundant, and more balanced and more constructive, from their perspective. Then you can talk with them about the ramifications of *that*. You may even find it beneficial to talk about several options and leave it up to them as to what they want to do. It's their free will as to whether they follow the old pattern—which some people do, even if they themselves consider it to be nonproductive—or to look at one of the alternatives that you have suggested, or maybe to do some thinking on their own and come up with an option that you would never have thought of. But the important thing is that you have helped them to see a cause/effect relationship, helped them to understand the effects of their actions, and you've helped to give them recommendations on some alternate attitudes and courses of action. Then it's up to them to do as they wish with it. You have helped empower them by facilitating their seeing the power of choice in their lives! They can then choose to continue focusing on an opportunity rather than living with fear over a "problem." At the same time, the opportunity is present for you to be completely neutral as to what they decide to do.

Once a reader was talking to an individual who had some very unproductive patterns which were leading to the deterioration of the physical body. The reader indicated that if this pattern continued, it was quite possible that the individual would die. The individual was asked if they wanted to change the pattern. The individual said, "No." In fact, very soon thereafter the individual did cross over. They knew that their actions could lead to the termination of their life, and they chose to continue those actions. At that point it is important to be totally and completely nonjudgmental and neutral about the information and the seeker's decision.

If you pass on the information to the best of your ability, and have been in tune and balanced, then you've done your part. Your responsibility is fulfilled, and your conscience must be allowed to clear. What the individual does with the information from there on out is *their* business. Don't interfere. Remember that you cannot take responsibility for the seeker's life or choices. Your job is to act as a catalyst, to assist in the process of self-realization, but without becoming involved in the reaction yourself, and without being drained.

Do not be concerned if you get a different interpretation for a card every time you read. Likewise, do not be concerned if the interpretation you feel is correct is different from the interpretation for the card found in this or any other book. If you find that your attention in a reading is drawn to different details or things within the card itself, allow this information to come through—it is one of the reasons that you chose a deck with vivid pictures. The pictures on the cards give you more to work with. Remember, go with your first impressions and your first thoughts. Trust yourself, and believe that you know.

What if you get absolutely *no* impressions from the card? There are five things you can do if this happens:

1. First, don't panic. Relax, take a deep breath, and make sure that your channel with the Higher Self is open.
2. Describe the card and the suit. Talk about what this card stands for (here is where a generalized knowledge of the suits and numerological aspects will come in handy).
3. Describe the details of the card, and look at the card. Notice small details you may have passed up before. Be attentive to the areas and items that your eyes are drawn to.
4. Touch the card. The cards themselves will hold vibrations. This is particularly helpful if the seeker has handled the cards. Allow this energy to come through,

whether it is in the form of visual pictures, or feelings, or actual knowledge.

5. Finally, you can say that you are not picking up anything on this card right now, so you will come back to it later. Relax, release the picture, and move on to another card, allowing your thoughts on these other cards to come through. Often a card will have more significance after you read some other cards.

It may be that your client is blocking the flow of information—watch their body language. This may just not be a good day to read for this person.

Reading for yourself is the hardest, because you are the least detached. In general, the closer the person is to you, the harder it is, because your conscious mind may color the information so that it meets what you believe they will accept. Often it is easier to read for a stranger.

Don't forget to record the readings. And another suggestion: consider getting a spiral notebook with one page per card. Write down your impressions on each card from every reading. If you have done this, then when you get stumped, you can go to your *own* book to reference your own impressions on the cards, not someone else's. And since what you are working with are your own impressions, these impressions are going to be more valid for you.

When you first get started, read for friends. Tell them that you are just beginning to read the cards, and that you want to read for them just for fun. This will take the pressure off of you and them. Even so, still record the readings. Then go back after a couple of months and find out what you were right or erroneous about, and fine tune your readings. You may be surprised that some of these early readings will be surprisingly good.

You may want to clear the cards after every reading. Just as you use grounding to clear yourself, you can use grounding to clear your cards. To do this,

> Hold the cards between both hands, palms flat, the heels of your hands close to your heart vortex (which is in the center of your chest). Visualize white light coming out from your heart into the cards. This clears them.

As with all things, follow your intuition. Just remember that the cards are only a tool. There is no special way or special place in which the cards should be kept—just put them where you can find them. Specifically, they do not need to be wrapped in cloth, or put in a wooden box, or slept with, or any other such superstitious advice. The power to use the cards constructively comes from you, not them. It is amazing how well the cards fit and travel in the box in which they were originally packed, which is where Richard's cards are kept.

12

LAYOUTS AND READINGS

The following information is presented from Richard's perspective, as he approaches reading for another person, but it is equally valid in reading for yourself or others.

In a private consultation, I go from a general reading to one or more specific readings in which I focus on specific questions.

Before the general reading, I focus and still the mind, calm the emotions, and relax the body through deep breathing techniques. I feel myself becoming lighter and connecting with my spiritual source (see the "Opening a Channel to the God-Self" and "Guided Meditation" sections for directions). At this time some initial guidance may come through. Then I open my eyes and say to the seeker,

"I seek to be a clear channel, allowing information to come through that will help you to help yourself. I know that that information will come through from the greatest and highest source possible and be presented in the most understandable fashion for you. All guidance given will deal with areas which you wish to work with and are prepared to work with. This consultation is being done in alignment with the greatest and highest good for all concerned."

I then ask if the seeker feels comfortable with this. If they say yes (which they always have!), then we have mutually set an energy pattern through a prayer or projection. The reading's context has now been set. (See the importance of clarity of mind?) I ask the seeker, for the purpose of this general reading, to keep their mind open when they shuffle and choose the cards, and to avoid having anything particular in mind. While they are shuffling, I am deciding which spread to use and sensing how many cards the seeker should select. (The Celtic Cross spread is great for the general reading.) I focus on keeping myself centered and relaxed at this time, and then lay out the cards.

This spread usually reveals the one or two major focuses that will help the seeker most in their growth. The specific readings usually show how this energy is expressing. As we look at the major areas of career, finances, relationships, and health (in specific spreads), we see how the major themes play out in their life. This gives the seeker an opportunity to clearly see cause/effect relationships and how their inner world affects their outer world. The advantage of this perception is that it allows them to understand that by transforming the one or two thoughts, belief systems, or attitudes revealed in the general reading, many of the questions which they have about career, finances, relationships, health, etc. will automatically resolve with time.

After the general reading is completed, we are ready to move on to the specific readings. I ask the person to start with the area which is uppermost on their minds. At this point, I have them ask me a specific question about the issue. Sometimes, I rephrase the question to refocus it, but again, I always work from the general to the specific. While their attention is thus directed, I have them shuffle again, and pick the number of cards which I would like to work with in that spread. This number varies according to the type of spread with which I want to work, and any intuitive impulses.

After that reading is finished, other questions may come up concerning information that surfaced within the specific reading. If I feel that it will be beneficial, I may choose to do yet another spread on these questions about the specific issue.

Often, at this point, my connection with the Higher Self is so open that I don't even need to use the cards, as impressions immediately come to mind. If this is the case, I will present whatever information I pick up. This may satisfy the client. At this point, if the seeker wants additional information, or I do, we may choose some additional cards.

When the seeker feels comfortable with whatever information has come through, we move on to the next issue, working again from the general information received to the specific question. In this way, we may deal with a number of issues.

There are many ways to choose the cards. If any particular method works for you, then fine. However, my preference is to allow the seeker to shuffle the cards until they feel right to the seeker, at which time he spreads the entire deck out in a fan across the table. I then ask the seeker to draw cards from the deck. The cards which are chosen will not necessarily be found one right behind the other. But if the seeker is sensitive, they will pull the right cards.

Do not shuffle the cards like a regular deck of cards—this breaks the backs down. Instead, hold the cards in one hand, and cut them with the other hand, dropping small groups of the cards into the front, in much the same way as children must shuffle cards before their hands are large enough to shuffle with both hands.

Additionally, if you shuffle in this manner, the cards will not be turned around. I am aware that some books read the cards reversed, and give different significance to the meanings depending on whether the cards are right side up, or reversed—but this means twice the number of meanings to remember and deal with. And then the question arises: reversed from whose perspective—yours, or the seeker who is sitting across from you? Shuffle the cards so that none of the cards are reversed. Then if a card gets turned around, you know that the seeker and their subconscious took the card and turned it around. The fact that the card is reversed now has significance. It may mean the opposite of what the card means right side up, or it may imply a lessening of the right-side-up quality.

As your client draws their cards, have them place these cards face down, one on top of the next. At this point, I usually pull my own cards. The number of cards that I will draw varies, usually three, but sometimes only two. On occasion, I have been known to pull ten cards of my own. Set your cards to the side. Now, take the stack of cards that your client has drawn, and bring them to you, making sure that the cards will be read right side up from your perspective. The card at the bottom is card #1, so go back through the cards and re-stack them, so that the last card drawn now becomes the card on the bottom, etc. Lay out the cards from your perspective. After reading this spread, see how the cards you selected fit in.

Now let's look at the different spreads.

SPREADS

THE CELTIC CROSS

Have the client draw ten to twelve cards. Now draw your cards, generally one to three.

Notice that there is no significator used. For those of you who have not read before, some readers use a single, separate card chosen before the shuffling begins to represent the seeker as a significator. I do not see the benefit in removing a card which may have more significance if it turns up in the reading.

Instead, when laying out the Celtic Cross, use Cards 1 and 2 to provide a point of focus into the core of the situation, since Card 2 is affecting the energy in Card 1, for better or for worse. In a general reading, these cards may also be used to provide

The Celtic Cross

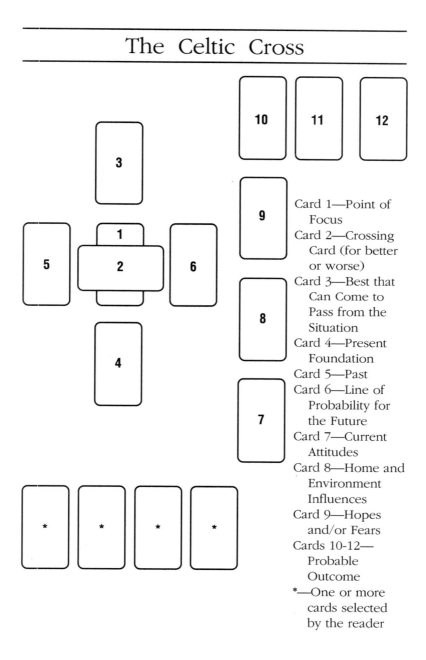

Card 1—Point of Focus

Card 2—Crossing Card (for better or worse)

Card 3—Best that Can Come to Pass from the Situation

Card 4—Present Foundation

Card 5—Past

Card 6—Line of Probability for the Future

Card 7—Current Attitudes

Card 8—Home and Environment Influences

Card 9—Hopes and/or Fears

Cards 10-12— Probable Outcome

*—One or more cards selected by the reader

Time Line Pyramid (variation 1)

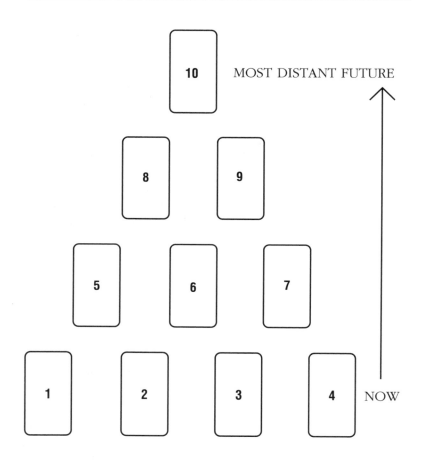

insight into the person in general, and their present focus. In a specific reading, use these two cards to provide insight into the person's focus regarding that question.

Look at the number of Major Arcana cards. There are twenty-two Major Arcana cards out of the seventy-eight total. This means that an average number would be two to three. The Major Arcana deal with major opportunities, major lessons—the big things. If four or more Major Arcana cards appear, the client is probably going through major changes or has major opportunities/challenges.

Now, look at the cards you have drawn and see how they fit with the client's cards. They could be dealing with how the energy may change with time, clarification of issues raised in the Celtic Cross, or amplification of a specific card in the spread. Just look at the cards you have drawn and see what comes to you.

TIME LINE PYRAMID (variation 1)

Draw ten cards. Lay these cards out so that the first card drawn goes on 1, etc.

The Time Line Pyramid gives you lines of probability extending into the future. The bottom four cards deal with now, or possibly the recent past (remember that time slips a little when you deal with the subconscious mind). If it seems to deal with the recent past, then the next row of three cards would be the present. The farther you go up the levels, the farther into the future you are going. You may decide that each row represents a three-month period. Realize that time is very fluid; therefore, as you move up the pyramid, exact timing becomes more difficult. Also, some events depend upon other events. For instance, a person wanting to buy a car may need a pay raise before making a down payment. If an expected pay raise is delayed by three months, the car purchase will likely be delayed by three months.

If you feel like you are dealing with past-life limitations, you may want to draw some cards to get a better sense of what is limiting the seeker now.

The repetition of any numbers in this or any other spread is significant. Let your intuition tell you why those numbers are important.

TIME LINE PYRAMID (variation 2)

Draw eleven cards as you normally do. In this variation, card 1 represents the past, cards 2,3,4, and 5 represent the present. Cards 6,7, and 8 represent the future. Cards 9 and 10 represent the more distant future, and card 11 represents the even more distant future.

As with variation 1, it is important to recognize that the lines of probability become more hazy and thus predictions are more difficult to make the farther one goes into the future.

TIME LINE LAYOUT

In this layout, Card 1 is the first card to the reader's left, and successive cards are laid out beside one another, going to the right. With this layout, as with the two PYRAMID layouts, you select how far into the future you want to go—days, weeks, months, etc. Again, the farther away from the present you go, the less distinct the lines of probability become.

Cards 1, 2, and 3 will represent the present, or the past. Successive cards will go into the future. You may pick however many cards your intuition directs.

Time Line Pyramid (variation 2)

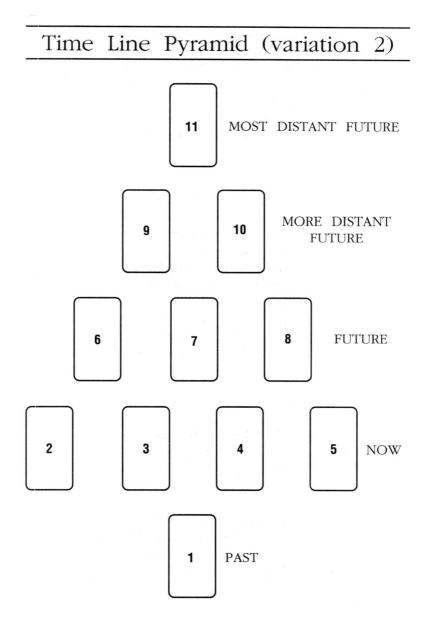

11 MOST DISTANT FUTURE

9 **10** MORE DISTANT FUTURE

6 **7** **8** FUTURE

2 **3** **4** **5** NOW

1 PAST

Time Line Layout

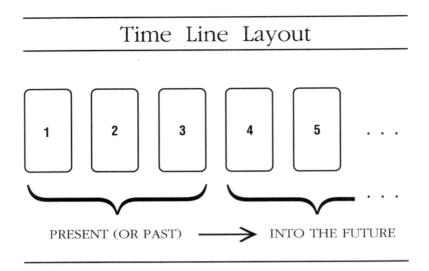

PRESENT (OR PAST) ⟶ INTO THE FUTURE

ONE OR MORE CARDS FOR CLARIFICATION:

One or more cards can be used as a spread. For instance, the seeker may have several job prospects. Two or three cards may be selected representing each option. Potential opportunities and pitfalls can be recognized by comparing the energy pattern associated with each prospect. The seeker can then make a more informed choice.

At times, confusion arises over how to interpret a card in a spread. If so, ask for clarification and select one or two cards. If a particular energy is being used in an unbalanced way, select a card knowing that it will provide insight into balancing the energy.

You may also select several cards with no specific expectations. If drawn for this reason, allow your intuition to tell you how to use the cards. In addition to the above mentioned uses, you may create a Time Line spread.

ONE OR MORE CARDS FOR PERSONAL USE

For meditation, a single card may be chosen in the morning or preceding evening to provide a point of focus for the day. If you are experiencing a conflict, select one or more cards for insight into its resolution. When faced with a challenge, I usually pull cards to answer these questions: What do I have to teach? What do I have to learn? What is my best focus? What is the opportunity? Answers to these questions are helpful in most any matter.

ORDER OF THE SPREADS

Do a general spread first, then go to specific ones.

For the general spread, I use the Celtic Cross.

For spreads on more specific issues, I will use one or more Celtic Cross layouts and, in addition, may use any one of the following: Time Line Pyramid, Time Line Layout, or the One or More Card Spread.

Always deal with general questions first, followed by more specific questions. After one question is dealt with, proceed to the next issue. Many specific questions are answered or at least addressed in the general reading, which helps to frame or provide an overall perspective for the seeker. In a general spread, several issues may come up. Basically, you are looking for overall trends and anything significant that pops up. Then you and the seeker will pick topics for subsequent spreads.

This format will help to point out cycles and how they show up in each area of a person's life—romance, home, job, finances, etc. Also, cause/effect relationships surface. If an old pattern is no longer productive, show them how a new cause can generate a new result. Chapter 14 on "Example Spreads" shows how these different layouts are used together in a consultation.

Carry on a conversation with the seeker. Ask the seeker if they have any questions or comments. It is particularly important to ask if the reading is clear for them. If it is not, then address any areas which are unclear.

What if someone does a reading for you and you disagree with their interpretation? Then ask them for their insights and impressions. *You* may not want to see, or they may be wrong. Listen, but use your own discretion. Trust yourself.

And remember, everything is only a line of probability. All of life is subject to change. Use of the Tarot leads to wiser choices which result in more productive changes.

13

SUGGESTED MEANINGS
FOR THE CARDS

The cards are arranged in numerical order, starting with the Major Arcana, and then moving through the suits of Wands, Swords, Cups, and Pentacles. The astrological significance of each Major Arcana card is given, and the numerological significance of each card is discussed in addition to possible interpretations. *Recognize that any card can mean anything in the context of a spread. The meanings given are a starting point. Follow your own intuition!!!*

When a card comes up, it may mean either that the quality embodied by the card is being used well, and in balance, or it may indicate that it is being used out of balance. If the latter, it indicates a need to place more attention on this area. A reversed card can imply a lessening of how it would be interpreted upright or the opposite of the upright card interpretation.

0
THE FOOL

Zero is complete—no end, and no beginning.

This card represents the planet, Uranus.

"You cannot enter heaven unless you have the faith of a little child." The faith of the child is represented by The Fool. This is the willingness to take a risk and follow your intuition even though you don't know the outcome. Joy and excitement, or foolhardiness and naiveté.

Notice that the sun, rose, and dog are white. This does not represent the physical sun, but the light of the inner being, the top of the inner triangle, enlightenment. The Fool has one step in front of him and then the great abyss. He is operating on faith as he steps into the unknown.

1
THE MAGICIAN

One is the beginning of a cycle. It is a masculine or assertive number, dealing with creation, will power, independence, and leadership.

This card represents the planet, Mercury.

Notice the rod in his right hand. This represents the connection with the God-Self. The index finger of the left hand is pointing down, representing concentration, focused creative force, or the ability to cause change. On the table before him are the four signs: the wand, sword, cup, and pentacle. These represent the elements of fire, air, water, and earth; or the spiritual, mental, emotional, and physical planes. When you have the kind of focus represented by this card, with the connection to the God-Self, you have the ability to create in all realms—spiritual, mental, emotional, and physical.

Thus, he is able to manifest abundantly in all ways. He has the sign for infinity above his head. This signifies the connection with infinite power. This card deals with the conscious mind, concentration, and the ability to cause change. Creation of what is wanted can occur only through sufficient concentration.

This card can come up for an individual who has good focus and concentration, or for one whose attention is scattered and needs more focus.

2
THE HIGH PRIESTESS

Two is a feminine number which expresses the qualities of love, harmony, and kindness. One goes out, two receives. Two also deals with duality, choice, polarity, balance, and cooperation.

This card represents the Moon, whose light is the reflected light of the Sun.

The High Priestess can be a very reflective card, representing the power of the subconscious mind as it receives and reflects the desires of the conscious mind. After decisions are made, the subconscious begins to manifest, and then the challenge is to become receptive. Receptivity requires inner stillness. The soft blue and white colors convey this feeling. Look and listen to opportunities coming to you.

The letters B/J represent the yin and yang—the balance of masculine and feminine, or assertive and receptive. This card can appear for an individual who is very intuitive, psychic, and/or sensitive; or for one who needs to still the mind to receive these qualities.

THE EMPRESS.

3
THE EMPRESS

Three is the number of joy,
creation, abundance, imagination,
and artistic expression.
When you combine the masculine
(1) and the feminine (2), you
form what is created (3).

This card represents the planet,
Venus.

Notice the tremendous abundance in this card: stars in
the hair, wheat fields in the front, forest and waterfall in the
back. These elements represent abundance, prosperity, or the
ideal picture of woman. This card may appear when we are
feeling good about ourselves and/or when projects dear to us
are nearing completion.

THE EMPEROR.

4
THE EMPEROR

Four is the number of stability,
just as four legs on a chair give
the chair stability.
It is also the number of
organization, structure, work,
discipline, and order.

This card represents the
astrological sign, Aries.

Just as The Empress represents an idealized representation of woman, this card presents an idealized representation of man.

The Emperor sits on a concrete throne, symbolizing great stability, leadership, and order. The primary color is red, which can be a call to action. The golden crown, ankh, and orb represent wisdom, life, and authority.

This card can appear for a person who has good logic, reasoning, analytical skills, and a very structured environment.

5
THE HIEROPHANT

Five is the number of freedom, progress, change, courage, and versatility.

This card represents the astrological sign, Taurus.

The Hierophant is a pope or a religious leader. He represents the God within, the superconscious mind, or the inner teacher who always has a firm footing which can help us gain truth. Notice he is standing on a cube with two keys affixed to the front. The cube represents truth which can be opened with the keys of spiritual wisdom. The gesture of his right hand shows that he is not presenting all of the answers, but rather, what he perceives as truth.

This card may appear for a spiritual teacher, an individual devoted to right personal development, or to someone whose arrogance has stunted their spiritual growth.

6
THE LOVERS

Six is the number of service, truth, responsibility, and love of home and family.

This card represents the astrological sign, Gemini.

In the picture, the man, representing the conscious mind, looks to the woman, who represents the subconscious mind, and she in turn looks to the angel, who represents the superconscious mind, for guidance. This is a symbolic representation of the process of opening up to your God-Self. Through inner communication and alignment between the male and female selves, wisdom naturally flows from your Higher Self. "If thine eye be singular, thy body shall be full of light"—this card represents the "marriage made in heaven," the inner marriage.

This card may indicate a strong soul connection or romance between two people, in addition to great inner attunement.

7
THE CHARIOT

Seven is the number of
spirituality, wisdom, and
synthesis. Seven's power comes
from silence and inner
attunement.

This card represents the
astrological sign, Cancer,
and can highlight issues about
one's home.

Notice the black and white sphinx; they represent the *yin* and the *yang,* or balance. The chariot's symmetry also emphasizes balance. Notice that the Charioteer has no reins—the chariot is directed by the mind. With the stars in the crown and canopy, this card can represent opportunities appearing.

Egyptian symbology abounds. As a result, this card may appear when an individual is receiving information from the Mystery Schools (Egyptian or otherwise) or tapping into past-life memories.

8
STRENGTH

Eight is the number of giving and
receiving in balance, which leads
to power, authority,
success, and material fortune.

This card represents the
astrological sign, Leo.

Note the infinity sign appears again, signifying the
potential of linking with the God-Self. This linkage can only
occur when we operate from our inner strength, a quality
represented here. In this card, the woman works with the lion,
governing his strength through love and gentleness. This is the
same way that we deal with the powerful energies within
ourselves. This card can also represent activating our powerful
creative energy, called *kundalini,* with loving control.

An individual experiencing inner strength or *kundalini*
energy movement may see this card in a spread. On the other
hand, this card can appear when one can use additional
confidence or clarity.

9
THE HERMIT

Nine is the last number in the first cycle. It is the number of completion, brotherhood, and Universal Love.

This card represents the astrological sign, Virgo.

The Hermit signifies the end of a cycle. In the pattern of growth, the last step is to teach what you know. If you cannot teach it, you don't have a good grasp of the concepts. Notice that the Hermit is at the top of his mountain, but that there is no room for anyone else. The wise teacher recognizes that his or her path is unique and that their job is merely to act as a catalyst to enable others to find their own truth and journey to the top of their own mountain.

The staff is the mark of a teacher. He leans out over the abyss, and shines the light of spiritual awareness for everyone else to see. Notice the six-pointed star which serves as the light inside the lantern. The six points represent the service provided through sharing wisdom. This star is made up of a triangle pointing up and a triangle pointing down, signifying the quality of spirit coming into matter. Its golden color represents wisdom. His grey robes are neither black nor white, but a balanced blending of both, emphasizing a teacher's balance.

10
WHEEL OF FORTUNE

Ten is 1 + 0. 1 is the beginning of a new cycle, and 0 represents the completion of a previous cycle. This signifies the application of wisdom gained in the previous cycle to a new one. Although it may seem like you are back at the same point, you aren't, because you have grown through the earlier cycle.

This card represents the planet, Jupiter.

This card signifies growth, evolution, and karma, and can represent the understanding of cause and effect. Notice the snake evolving into the jackal evolving into the sphinx. Also notice the four corners: the man, eagle, lion, and bull. These symbols represent the four planes of existence: mental, emotional, spiritual, and physical. This card expresses the opportunity to create on all planes with understanding.

This card may appear when an individual is working through a karmic situation or is experiencing a period of rapid growth.

11
JUSTICE

Eleven is a master number.
It is the number of teaching
spiritual truth,
or being a spiritual light
messenger.

This card represents the
astrological sign, Libra.

This card signifies divine balance, divine justice, and the importance of not going to extremes. The law is exacting. As you sow, so shall you reap.

This card can surface when an individual seeks balance, is rearranging their priorities, or is facing a legal situation. Additionally, with eleven being the spiritual light messenger, Justice may appear for a person who aspires to create planetary balance through sharing a spiritual message.

12
THE HANGED MAN

The number of The Hanged Man, 12, reduces to a 3 (1 + 2). Three is the number of joy, creation, abundance, and artistic expression.

This card represents the planet, Neptune.

This card represents a person going their own way, doing what they know to be best. It represents inner confidence, regardless of anybody else's point of view.

Notice the contented expression on this man's face. When you are operating from your own inner truth, it doesn't matter what the rest of the world thinks about you. If you're doing what you are supposed to, and you are happy, you are on your correct path. This is the person marching to the beat of a different drummer. The halo represents tremendous inner peace and contentment. Sometimes this card appears when an individual is "running with the crowd," and it is time for them to express more of their uniqueness.

13
DEATH

The number of Death, 13, reduces to a 4 (1 + 3). Four is the number of stability, organization, structure, work, discipline, and order.

This card represents the astrological sign, Scorpio.

Death signifies major change. The only way that you can become more at one with God is to grow through change, releasing the limitations of the past and embracing new opportunities. This card could also signify the death of the Piscean Age, and the coming of the Aquarian Age. The sun rising on the horizon signifies great promise and rebirth.

This card may appear for an individual going through tremendous transformation, or a person who is resisting change.

14
TEMPERANCE

The number of Temperance, 14, reduces to a 5 (1 + 4). Five is the number of freedom, progress, change, courage, and illumination.

This card represents the astrological sign, Sagittarius.

Temperance signifies balance through moderation and harmonization.

Notice that she has one foot in the water and one on land, signifying balance. The sun rising on the horizon signifies promise. The wings may represent the process of rising above limitations by finding the balance in it, or touching the Higher Self.

Balance in all things, and nothing to an extreme, leads to a joyous, happy life.

THE DEVIL .

15
THE DEVIL

The number of The Devil, 15, reduces to a 6 (1 + 5). Six is the number of service, truth, devotion, and idealism.

This card represents the astrological sign, Capricorn.

Set the card of The Hierophant next to the card of The Devil. Notice that The Hierophant is standing on a cube, The Devil on a half-cube. This represents truth vs. half-truths. Notice also the hands, and particularly the showing of the palms. The Hierophant signs, "I present what I perceive to be truth," while The Devil signs, "I know *all* the truth."

Notice that The Devil has donkey's ears, ram's horns, bat wings, and eagle talons. There are creatures that have each of these aspects, but there is no single creature that has all of these together. The significance of this is similar to gossip, i.e., having enough of the truth borrowed from here and there, but putting it together into a context which is not accurate.

Notice the chains around the necks of the man and the woman, particularly that the chains are loose, and they could take the chains off of themselves. Thus the one who decides that they are unworthy can also decide that they are worthy.

This card represents gossip, self-limitations, an inferiority complex, being in a rut, ignorance and self-delusion—the facts may be true, but the conclusions are wrong. And "the truth shall make you free."

This is also an earth card. It may indicate dealing with earthy, practical things on the physical plane: power, possessions, money, sexuality. That is fine, as long as an obsession is not developed which overshadows our spiritual, mental, and emotional lives.

Starting with this card, and continuing through the next six cards to complete the Major Arcana, are the seven steps to spiritual enlightenment. In this context, The Devil represents a quality of being in despair.

THE TOWER.

16
THE TOWER

The number of The Tower, 16, reduces to a 7 (1 + 6). Seven is the number of spirituality, wisdom, and synthesis.

This card represents the planet, Mars.

The Tower represents an event which transforms your life—like the experience of Saul being struck by lightning on the road to Damascus.

Major change can often be an impetus for growth. It can be pleasant or unpleasant. People who create major change get The Tower. If they decide not to move through the changes which they have initiated, then the universe will force movement, sometimes resulting in "unpleasant" situations. It *looks* like the universe did it to them, but it is only their own thoughts in motion. However, when you go with the change, it can result in pleasant and rapid growth. Remember that on the way to the ground, you have time to learn what happened, incorporate it, and land on your feet.

As the second step in spiritual development, The Tower represents the kick in the pants, the thing that gets us moving out of despair, or the rut which we have created. In most cases, the change will be very dramatic and intense. Once a person has embarked on this second step, they have a choice of getting stuck in a new rut, believing that they've got all the answers, thus falling back into the quality of The Devil card, or going forward into the quality of The Star.

THE STAR.

17
THE STAR

The number of The Star, 17, reduces to an 8 (1 + 7). Eight is the power and authority number, signifying success and material fortune.

This card represents the astrological sign, Aquarius.

The individual in this card is naked, and is pouring water from the pool onto the land, with stars above her head. This nakedness represents an acceptance of the self. Dipping into the pool represents meditation and inner attunement, and the potential for growth is symbolized by pouring water on the land. The stars in the sky portend opportunity.

As the third step in spiritual development, The Star represents acceptance of one's self, and dipping into the pool of wisdom which is within and which is found through meditation, inner attunement, and quiet time.

THE MOON.

18
THE MOON

The number of The Moon, 18, reduces to a 9 (1 + 8) Nine is the number of completion, brotherhood, and Universal Love.

This card represents the astrological sign, Pisces.

This represents getting in touch with the fruits of meditation, or new truths, and reflection. It can also reflect the surfacing of fears, anger, or other suppressed thoughts and feelings. Traditionally, this card has been viewed as dealing with psychic or occult experiences.

The lobster coming out of the water represents the surfacing of a thought, feeling, or experience. It can be the new awareness of insight, intuition, or spiritual experience. But it could also signify a suppressed, repressed, or unpleasant experience coming out to be dealt with and released.

With the lobster coming up out of the water and treading on a path between the domestic dog and the wolf, the focus is on balance, not being overly wild like the wolf, nor overly tame like the dog.

As the fourth step to spiritual enlightenment, The Moon represents the fruits coming forth from meditation and inner attunement.

19
THE SUN

The number of The Sun, 19,
reduces to a 1 (1 + 9 = 10 = 1).
One is the number of beginnings,
creation, will power,
independence, and leadership.

This card represents the Sun.

This is the most joyous and happy card in the deck! A sense of freedom, joy, and happiness is exuded by the child and expressed by the sun and sunflowers. The horse represents will power, and the naked child represents acceptance of our childlike nature, which in reality is our God-Self. Remember, "Truly, I tell you, whoever does not receive the kingdom of God as a little child will never enter it" (Mark 10:15).

As the fifth step to spiritual enlightenment, The Sun represents a recognition of your God-Self, that joyous, happy child which is your true identity.

20
JUDGMENT

The number of Judgment, 20, reduces to a 2 (2 + 0 = 2). Two is the number of love, harmony, receptivity, duality, polarity, balance, and cooperation.

This card represents the planet, Pluto.

In this card, naked people are rising out of graves in response to the trumpet of the angel. In The Death card, death represents change. In this card, the people are coming up out of the death state, which represents a major change in how one's self is viewed. They are naked, so they are viewing themselves honestly. They are grey, which indicates a quality of balance, and they are responding to the calling of the Angel, which represents the calling of the God-Self. So what you have here are the aspects of the individual going through change, rising up out of the limitations of the past, and responding to the calling of the God-Self. Through change you are reborn, rising above the limitations of the past, and preparing to move forward.

This card also governs the judgment of the self—not dealing with yourself harshly because of the mistakes of the past, but realizing that the mistakes were born of ignorance. Therefore, they cannot operate to limit your rebirth after you have forgiven yourself. It also signifies rising above the restraints of *karma* and the mental and emotional ties of the world through forgiveness and love—being in the world, but not of the world.

As the sixth step to spiritual enlightenment, Judgment represents the resurrection and bringing to the fore your true identity in response to the call of the Angel, who is the superconscious mind, or the God-Force.

21
THE WORLD

The number of The World, 21, reduces to a 3 (2 + 1 = 3). Three is the number of joy, creation, abundance, and artistic expression.

This card represents the planet, Saturn.

The wreath, shaped in a circle, represents completion in itself, no endings, and no beginnings. This card represents the end of a higher cycle, and the culmination of all the previous cards from 0 to 21. Mastery over all planes of experience—mental, emotional, spiritual and physical—is expressed by the man, eagle, lion, and bull found in the corners. Having incorporated all the lessons and changes available there, the next step is to return to the new cycle, The Fool, carrying with you all of the understandings of the past cycle. The Fool creates a bridge back to the Magician and the beginning of a new cycle. Thus The World card ends the Major Arcana with a promise of new experiences, adventures, and growth.

The World represents the seventh, and final step to spiritual enlightenment: achieving cosmic consciousness, which is consistently operating from your true identity, God-Self. Operating from the higher vibrations serves to raise the vibrations of the world and the people around you, making their path to greater awareness easier. Thus, like The Hermit, the achievement of mastery is shared with others. But The

Hermit, having reached individual spiritual enlightenment, reaches to individuals. Those who have reached cosmic enlightenment reach out to help the whole world.

THE MINOR ARCANA

There are twenty-two cards in the Major Arcana. Numerologically, the 22 is a master number which represents the spiritual master builder.

Next are the fifty-six Minor Arcana cards. There are four "suits," if you will: Wands, Swords, Cups, and Pentacles. Wands deal with spirituality, and represent the elemental force of fire. Swords deal with mental processes and represent the elemental force of air. Cups deal with emotions and relationships, and represent the elemental force of water. Pentacles deal with the qualities of money, home, earthly possessions, and other manifestations on the physical plane. Pentacles represent the elemental force of earth.

As a side note, there is an alternative system which incorporates all five suits, and correlates these five suits to the *chakras* of the body. In this system, the Major Arcana cards represent spirituality and the Wands express the qualities of energy and power. There is no interpretational change with Swords, Cups, or Pentacles.

Additionally, the sequences within the Minor Arcana also symbolize the challenges or successes which may be encountered in each step of the process of learning to master manifestation. Briefly, the first step is to become attuned to your spiritual nature through opening a spiritual channel to the universe (Wands), then mentally choosing goals which are in harmony with the spiritual insight to be attracted (Swords), and clearly visualizing the essence of the thing which you desire. At that point, you power-up the request using your emotions (Cups). The final step is to remain receptive for the manifestation on the physical plane (Pentacles) and to give thanks.

Ones represent new beginnings, and deal with creation, will power, independence, and leadership.

ACE

Notice that all of these cards have the divine hand of God coming out of the clouds, with a gift. Aces represent new beginnings. The hand pictured *is* the hand of God, but not a capricious God, *i.e.*, you have caused this to happen; accept and rejoice in the new opportunities open to you. What you are seeing is your own energy cycling back to you.

ACE OF WANDS   Initiation into new aspects of the spiritual realm, or the experience of new energies.

ACE OF SWORDS   The beginning or birth of a new idea on the mental plane. This idea may be generated in your mind, or it may be another's idea that you put into action.

ACE OF CUPS   Remember that cups represent emotions. The picture here is of the dove coming down from heaven with the communion wafer in his mouth. This has spiritual implications, even though cups generally deal with the emotions and the emotional plane. The overflowing cup represents overflowing abundance or overflowing love, from which all other things spring. This Ace can represent a new relationship—love, friendship, or business.

ACE OF PENTACLES   This represents new beginnings on the physical plane—a new home, job, money, or other material opportunity. You may now be seeing the results of an idea acted upon days, weeks, months, or years ago.

Twos represent the qualities of love, harmony, cooperation, polarity, duality, choice, and balance. With two, the opportunity exists to deal with conflicts which have arisen and resolve that duality to create balance.

TWO

TWO OF WANDS   Here the picture is of a man with the world in the palm of his hand. We use this expression when a person has tremendous opportunity. After you realize that you have the world in the palm of your hand, and recognize that you have the power and the potential to direct a situation, the challenge is to decide what you are going to do with it. This question is resolved by the Three of Wands.

TWO OF SWORDS   Here the blindfolded woman holds a sword in either hand, her arms crossed in front of her. She cannot take the blindfold off until she chooses which sword to put down, until then she is willfully blind. This may represent being on the horns of a dilemma, or at a crossroads where you are indecisive. Note that making the decision may be more important than the choice chosen, since after the decision is made, movement (growth) is again possible. Are you mentally refusing to look at your options, or take a stand?

TWO OF CUPS   This is the traditional marriage card. It may also indicate the marriage made in heaven, or the spiritual marriage of masculine and feminine within the self, or a spiritual marriage between two people. Of course the higher spiritual interpretation is far more important than the more physical interpretation. Always look at a situation from the inside out—from the highest level to the lowest. As we create inner harmony, we tend to reflect that harmony in our relationships.

TWO OF PENTACLES   Another card of turmoil from indecision, this time on the physical plane. In this card, the ships are being tossed around on the sea, indicating quite a bit of turmoil while this person is juggling the pentacles. Is the individual able to handle a lot of things at the same time and keep them in balance, or is he trying to deal with so many things at once that he can't do any of them well?

THREE

 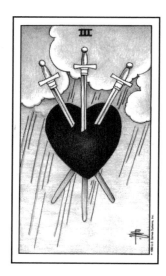

Three is a number of creation, abundance, imagination, joy, and artistic expression. It expresses the quality of building and creating.

THREE

THREE OF WANDS   Here the man stands on the mountain looking out across the water. His elevated vantage point provides him a great position from which to set the course of the ships, and thus create his reality. This is a perfect follow-through from the Two of Wands, and represents the third step: after the opportunity is given to you, and you recognize your potential to deal with it, you reach the third step which is the act of creation at the spiritual level: having the visionary quality, deciding what you are going to do with it, and taking action on it.

THREE OF SWORDS   This represents difficulties in your mental relationships—sadness and heartache with yourself, someone else, or a situation. This can arise as a result of a lack of focus, or a scattered focus. You have a choice for the future: you can either prioritize and focus on, for instance, three main things, trimming away the excess, or you can continue to scatter your attention and experience frustration. An unpleasant situation can be positively transformed by releasing your expectations or looking for the opportunity inherent within it. Nothing happens by chance. We have called to us every situation in our lives. In each one there is an opportunity to teach and learn. Find out how to turn a millstone into a milestone.

THREE OF CUPS   This card pictures the celebration of the harvest, with a high emotional quality to it. This ties in perfectly with the quality of the threes, which is creation. This may be the celebration of great abundance and prosperity, as when a new job, promotion, or a wonderful new relationship has come up, and you are celebrating the joy and happiness in it. But this card, picturing the women, each drinking from a cup, could also be indicative of drug or alcohol abuse (the false celebration).

THREE OF PENTACLES   This card shows an individual holding a blueprint, and another individual with a hammer and chisel in hand. Having developed a blueprint in your mind of what you want to create, you are going out and making it—the follow through necessary to bring an idea into complete physical manifestation.

FOUR

Fours deal with the qualities of organization, structure, discipline, work, and order.

FOUR

FOUR OF WANDS   In this card a feast or celebration is going on. The picture portrays a pastoral scene, being outside, and may represent getting back to nature. This card represents stability and order in the spiritual which can filter through to the physical plane. It may indicate a marriage in the future.

FOUR OF SWORDS   The picture in this card is of a tomb, with a stained glass window behind it. There are three swords on the wall which may represent trophies, and as such, indicate the successful completion of projects, personal transformations, or conflict resolution. This card may either indicate change coming, or that the person is now coming to a time of mental resting and regrouping following completion of something important in their lives. The stained glass window and the hands in the prayer position lend an air of reverence.

FOUR OF CUPS   Have you asked the universe for something? Here the man stares intently at the three cups before him, and from out of the clouds comes a hand holding a gift, which looks just like the Ace of Cups. But are you so busy looking at the cups before you that you don't see the opportunity coming? If so, perhaps you have gotten stuck in a rut and fail to recognize the divine opportunity being offered to you in an unexpected way. If, on the other hand (no pun intended), you open your vision to a broader experience of life, the new cup (opportunity) is clearly visible and within easy reach. This card may also represent the qualities obtained through meditation—and that through meditation unlimited opportunities come to you, sometimes in unexpected ways.

FOUR OF PENTACLES   Here the man is tightly clutching his pentacles. Is this a greedy individual, or does he have good reason to be holding onto his money? Is he in a situation where he is afraid that people either will take advantage or have been taking advantage of him? Is he a miser? Notice that the pentacle is held over his chest and solar plexus—the love and power centers—standing on two more, and the fourth is attached to his crown. Is he using his material abundance to help enhance the flow in these areas, or is he so concerned about money that he is shutting down on all other levels, thus blocking the flow in each of these areas?

Five is the number of freedom, progress, change, courage, and versatility.

FIVE

FIVE OF WANDS   In this picture the children can either be playing or fighting. This is representative of the inner spiritual struggles, wherein the various aspects of the self either work with or against each other, creating situations in which you allow ideas to play out in order to come to good decisions, or a battle on a spiritual level which creates havoc in your life to allow you an opportunity to grow.

FIVE OF SWORDS   This indicates the process of picking up the pieces after some struggle, either an internal or external one. Does this man have a smug expression? If so, perhaps others will resent him being a poor winner and look to "get even" later.

FIVE OF CUPS   Here the man focuses on the three cups that are spilled, not the two cups which still remain. This is an emotional decision—deciding whether or not to continue to cry over spilled milk. But if you continue to focus on what you don't have, you will not be able to make use of what you do have. This card can come up after a person has gone through a heartache, the loss of a relationship, or some other form of sadness. Remember that every situation, no matter how painful, holds within it an opportunity. Releasing the old makes way for accepting the new.

FIVE OF PENTACLES   This is a very interesting card. There is a bit of a dichotomy here—the two beggars are out in the snow, in destitute circumstances and physical hardship, but you also have the beautiful stained glass window shining in the night, offering a spiritual haven. So, like the Five of Cups, it depends on where you place your attention: you can either focus on the two poor souls, creating hard times in order to learn from the process of adversity, wounding, or sacrifice, or recognize that right around the corner is the door to a new spiritual enlightenment, or a much more optimistic opportunity. The church represents the opportunity of finding your truth within. The freedom of choice is yours.

SIX

Six is the number of service, truth, responsibility, and love of home and family.

SIX

SIX of WANDS   Here the man is returning. Is he victorious? The laurel wreath is indicative of victory or success, but look at the face of the man at the far left. Notice that this man is in the position, and has the means, to hit the rider. His facial expression may indicate dissatisfaction. Does the card represent a true victory, or merely the appearance of a victory, after which you are about to be blindsided?

This is the card of spiritual service—look at your intentions and what you want. Your intentions may determine whether your victory is lasting or short- lived.

SIX of SWORDS   This card shows a boatman poling a boat across an expanse of water, with a woman and child inside of it. The challenge with this card is to decide if you are represented by the woman, who is hooded, and appears to have gone through rough times, or the individual poling the boat. Look on the right side of the boat: the waves are rough, but on the left side the waves are smooth. If you identify with the woman, this card could indicate a passage through rough times, to the smoother waters, and the promised land beyond. If you identify with the one poling the boat, then it could indicate a person who is helping people over rough times. This card, being a sword, emphasizes service through thoughts, ideas, and plans; however, other forms of service are not excluded.

SIX of CUPS   Here the two little hobbits seem to indicate unconditional love and compassion. But is this love, or the illusion of love—a luring into a false emotional situation by the appearance of love and the presentation of gifts? This card can represent the giving or receiving of emotional support.

SIX of PENTACLES   This card shows scales in balance. Is this someone who is so abundant on the physical plane that they give it to others, in service to humanity? Is it given freely, or as a manipulation? Is this the quality of handing out justice? or *karma* on the physical plane, *i.e.,* whatever goes around, comes around? Do you relate to the person giving, receiving, or just watching?

99

SEVEN

Seven is the number of spirituality, wisdom, and synthesis.

SEVEN

SEVEN OF WANDS   This card shows a man on top of a hill; perhaps there are people below him holding staffs. Is he leading them, or fighting with them? Either way, he is in a superior position. A friend of Richard's interprets this card as the "Yes, do it!" card. It might not necessarily be easy, but you've got the position, and the opportunity, so take the ball and run with it. The spiritual synthesis is now complete, and the time to take action has come.

SEVEN OF SWORDS   This can indicate a balancing act, or a warning to be careful. Here the man holds an armful of swords in a precarious manner, and is obviously walking on tiptoe. Is he picking up the swords, or carefully inserting them? Look at the people on the horizon—is he stealing the swords while they are unaware? Or are you stealing from yourself? Perhaps it is time to get your ducks (swords) or ideas in a row.

SEVEN OF CUPS   Here the magician conjures up seven cups, with a different image coming out of each one. Is this illumination or illusion? This may indicate that things are not what they seem. Look at the bottom cup—is that a skull? And look at the face of the woman—is she confident, crafty, or contemplative?

This card can represent creativity and imagination. Here you see the range of possible manifestations as a result of your thoughts and emotions. As a man thinketh in his heart, so it is. Every thought (particularly one with feeling) will ultimately come back to you and be experienced in all areas of your life. Choose wisely!

SEVEN OF PENTACLES   Here the man leans on his hoe and gazes at the ripe pentacles hanging on their vine. Is he being indolent, or patient? Sometimes it is time to be patient: you sow the seeds and wait for the harvest. If you try to harvest too soon, the plants may be damaged and the fruit lost. But is he waiting to harvest, or refusing to take action although the time is right? This card can represent the importance of patience, or the folly of procrastination.

EIGHT

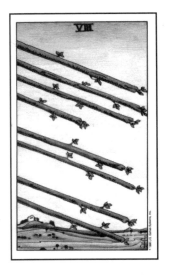

Eight is the number of giving and receiving in balance, which leads to power, success, and material fortune.

EIGHT

EIGHT OF WANDS   Here the staffs are parallel to each other, but the ends are not aligned. They seem to have a sense of order, but it is not yet complete. This could refer to a project moving towards completion (perhaps 80% - 90%), or that order is coming, but more work is needed.

EIGHT OF SWORDS   This card can represent self-binding limitation (notice the similarity with the Two of Swords). Recognize that if you find yourself in a limiting situation, somehow you have put yourself there, often as a result of negative thoughts. You created it, so you have the ability to release yourself. Once you have taken back your power, movement in any direction is possible. Notice that the person could back up against one of the swords, cut the bindings, and take *off* the blindfold. Thus, even now, they are free to go anywhere *they* choose.

EIGHT OF CUPS   Notice the order of the cups—all very neatly stacked one on top of the other. This may indicate that you have done a good job in one area or another, and that it is now time to move on. A cycle has come to an end, and it is time for a new adventure to begin.

EIGHT OF PENTACLES   This is the picture of a man who is making pentacles. He could be making money, or creating some other success on the physical plane. This card can also refer to a person with a lot of different talents (notice that all the pentacles look a little different).

NINE

Nine is the number of completion, brotherhood, and Universal Love.

NINE

NINE OF WANDS This is a picture of a man with a bandaged head after a battle. Through life we gain experiences and understandings, represented by the wands. Sometimes you get your nose bloodied, but you learn. Notice that the staves are behind him. It would be very difficult for an enemy to attack him from that quarter. He has a staff in his hand, and he looks like he can handle himself. Perhaps the wisdom gained from past situations will help him to avoid repeating the same mistakes again, and help him learn through an easier way in the future. But notice that the staff which he took in his hand is the one which belongs directly behind his back. Has he made himself vulnerable?

NINE OF SWORDS This card may refer to needless worries, anxiety, nightmares, or, *very rarely*, physical death. Notice that the quilt has a pattern—roses alternated with signs of the zodiac—which indicates great promise. Down in the bottom there appears to be a sword fight, but only one person appears to have a sword. Are you mentally creating your own problems, and needlessly worrying? Things may be better than you think—open your eyes and perceive your opportunities. You are covered by a beautiful and colorful quilt, just as we are surrounded by God's love.

NINE OF CUPS This is the traditional card of wish-fulfillment. Arrayed behind the man are nine cups, all equidistant from him. This may indicate tremendous opportunities around him—is he contemplating his options, or refusing to choose at all? Is he proud of what he has, or does he want too much? He does appear to be a bit overweight; perhaps he has been consuming too much. Is he a bit greedy or gluttonous? Here the man gets to choose—is he using what he has, or misusing it? Is he consuming what he has, or wasting it? Once again we see the importance of choice and attention.

NINE OF PENTACLES This is the card of abundance, the fruits of successful mastery of the lessons of physical manifestation. Here the lady in waiting is surrounded by great abundance. The card has a quality of completion and material happiness.

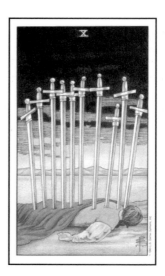

These are very intense cards, signifying new beginnings. The old cycle is completed and the new one begun with power, since you carry the wisdom or folly of the previous cycle.

TEN

TEN OF WANDS   This gentleman is carrying a great many wands. This can either represent having a great deal of understandings that you are bringing back with you, or it can refer to spiritual burdens, or being burdened by information that you have. Ignorance is bliss; with knowledge does come responsibility. Once we have knowledge, we sometimes feel burdened with the responsibility of what we are going to do with it.

TEN OF SWORDS   In this card, a man is lying face down in a pool of blood, with ten swords in his back. This may indicate a person who has hit bottom. The good news is that from the bottom, the only way is up. Notice that the sun is rising. This may be the return of hope. And look at his hand: he is making the same hand sign as The Hierophant; the sign of a blessing. This card can represent the need for forgiveness of yourself or another. Also, it may appear when it is time to release anything that is holding you back. Release thoughts, feelings, beliefs, relationships, jobs, material possessions, or anything else that is no longer beneficial.

TEN OF CUPS   This can be the card of emotional fulfillment: happiness, happy husband, wife, kids, house, the rainbow of promise—the idyllic vision of marriage and home life. But is this truth or illusion? Can reality measure up to this vision? Remember that you must accept your partner, family and friends as they are; they change themselves, not you.

TEN OF PENTACLES   This card shows an old man with his family in very abundant surroundings. This could refer to the person who has mastered material creation, earning its fruits— old age, wisdom, and great abundance. Or it could refer to a squandered abundance, or abundance which is not used to help others. Is this a person who has become so satisfied that he refuses to move further, and therefore is stagnating?

The Page indicates a person who is just starting in a new area, or children. A person could be ninety-six years old and have a page come up, indicating that they are starting anew in some area of life. These cards are often seen with Aces in a spread.

COURT CARDS can either represent an individual's level of awareness, or their age (child, adolescent, or adult).

PAGE

PAGE OF WANDS   This card expresses a great sense of wonder about spiritual matters. It may appear when a person has experienced a spiritual initiation, changed denominations or religions, or begun exploring new spiritual or religious paths.

PAGE OF SWORDS   This card conveys an eagerness to explore new ideas. It may appear when an individual has begun to develop new ideas or look at life in a new way.

PAGE OF CUPS   This card expresses an eagerness to explore the emotions which may carry the promise of spiritual development, as the fish is coming up out of the cup. The fish is the traditional symbol of Christianity. Also, this card may appear when new feelings surface or when a new relationship has begun.

PAGE OF PENTACLES   Notice the fascination with the pentacle, or manifestations, like a child with a flower. This card may appear when a person begins to implement a new idea or when tangible results from a project first appear.

These cards represent the period of trying out new ideas, while still making quite a few mistakes, just as adolescents do in their attempts to master maturity. These cards could also represent an adolescent.

KNIGHT

KNIGHT OF WANDS   Here is a person testing out the spiritual information given, and working towards an understanding that they don't yet have. Notice how energetic this horse is. Is the power being harnessed for good, or is it out of control?

KNIGHT OF SWORDS   Look at the details in this card: the young man is charging forward into what appears to be gale force winds (look at the trees). Notice the look of terror on the horse's face, and notice also that his legs are outstretched as if he were trying to stop. Remember that the horse represents the will. Is there an inner conflict in this pursuit for mental mastery? Or perhaps the problem is that he is unsure as to the direction—with the wind, or against it? Sometimes this card seems to mean that a person ought to go for it, and at other times it seems to indicate that the person is swimming upstream against the universal flow. Could you be facing resistance and simply need to persevere to succeed?

KNIGHT OF CUPS   Notice the wings on the helmet and shoes, reminiscent of the symbols associated with Hermes, the messenger god of the Greeks. Is this representative of intuitive or psychic ideas coming in, perhaps through the channel of the feelings? Or perhaps this is the good knight, the person bearing good ideas. Or it could be a person who insists on proper behavior. This card may also be an indication that issues of communication need to be dealt with.

KNIGHT OF PENTACLES   Notice the sense of heaviness in this card: heavy armor, a heavy horse. Contrary to the other Knights, this Knight conveys no sense of motion. This card could refer to something in the process of physical manifestation, or perhaps that your project will take longer to complete than you think. Maybe with a little more energy, you can get your project moving again.

QUEEN

Queens represent a great deal of receptive awareness, or an adult woman.

QUEEN

QUEEN OF WANDS   This card represents the quality of abundance, as a result of awareness and receptiveness to the spiritual. The holding of staff and sunflower could represent a balance between authority and sensitivity and love of beauty.

QUEEN OF SWORDS   This card may indicate a woman not to be crossed, or determination in the face of a challenge. Perhaps this is the same woman who sat blindfolded on the seashore in the Two of Swords, unwilling to choose or move. Now she has only one sword—having sought and found truth—and she holds it balanced and ready to take action. This card can represent a person with a sharp mind. The open left hand may represent a willingness to listen to new ideas and learn. The right hand holding a sword is indicative of singular focus and an ability to act upon it.

For women who feel manipulated or controlled, this is a good card for meditating on how to develop a more assertive nature.

QUEEN OF CUPS   Notice that the cup in this card is different from all the other cups in this suit. It bears more resemblance to a communion chalice than a drinking cup. The Queen pictured here exhibits a great deal of concentration. This card can represent a very sensitive person. The tranquility of the water and the multicolored pebbles at her feet can represent the peace of mind which comes from a concentrated mind going into meditation. However, does this woman's expression convey concentration or worry? If it is the latter, clarity of perception can be lost.

QUEEN OF PENTACLES   There is a great deal of abundance, as well as activity, around the Queen of Pentacles. Notice the flowers and the rabbit. This is a very earthy card, which has a feeling of the earth mother. This card can represent a person who very easily attracts material abundance.

Kings represent a great deal of awareness, combined with an assertive nature, or an adult man.

KING

KING OF WANDS   The King of Wands has a far off look in his eyes, perhaps indicating a visionary quality. This card can represent an individual who has great knowledge about spirituality and/or power and can convey it.

KING OF SWORDS   This King has a very penetrating glance, perhaps indicating great focus and concentration. There are a number of different images which can be seen in the throne above his head—perhaps a butterfly, or a charging bull. This card can represent an individual with a keen mind, who plans well, and/or has a great imagination. All of these fine mental qualities can be applied with mastery and precision.

KING OF CUPS   This King has a very small throne. There is a very unusual fish jumping out of the ocean to the left of the cup, and off to the right is a boat. Is this King about to be overtaken by the waves (possible emotional swings)? This card can represent a very caring, compassionate, and sensitive person who lovingly expresses these characteristics to others.

KING OF PENTACLES   This King wears a beautiful, long flowing robe with grapes, a symbol of abundance. Everything about this king expresses abundance. This card can represent an individual who has great material abundance, particularly one who shares abundance generously and is able to teach others how to create it in their own lives.

14

EXAMPLE SPREADS

Readings for Seeker #1

For these readings, we have used the Universal Waite deck. Please bear in mind that our intent is to include these readings only as illustrations. Feel free to develop your own interpretations or methods of reading. Every deck has different pictures and images which may modify the impressions that you get from the cards. The numerology and card suits are all that remain the same between one type of deck and the next. Shop around until you find the deck which best resonates with you.

There may be places in the following readings where the interpretations drawn from the cards have only a thin connection to the image, suit, or numerology of the cards showing. This extraneous information is an example of the type of intuitive flow (channeling) which occurs while reading the cards. It will feel to you like a hunch, a stray thought, or an urge to speak. Trust yourself, and speak it.

In the sample readings, you may want to lay out the actual cards being described to get a better "feel" for the interpretations.

SEEKER #1, READING #1

Celtic Cross Spread

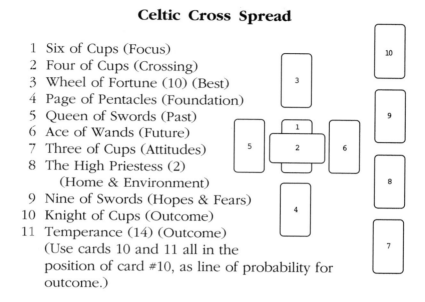

1 Six of Cups (Focus)
2 Four of Cups (Crossing)
3 Wheel of Fortune (10) (Best)
4 Page of Pentacles (Foundation)
5 Queen of Swords (Past)
6 Ace of Wands (Future)
7 Three of Cups (Attitudes)
8 The High Priestess (2)
       (Home & Environment)
9 Nine of Swords (Hopes & Fears)
10 Knight of Cups (Outcome)
11 Temperance (14) (Outcome)
     (Use cards 10 and 11 all in the
     position of card #10, as line of probability for
     outcome.)

Clarification Cards
* Strength (8)
* Five of Cups
* King of Wands
* The Moon (18)

    The first impression in this reading is a sense of move-
ment from ideas to action. The Queen of Swords, through the
Six and Four of Cups and through the Ace of Wands, conveys
a sense of movement, from ideas to feelings to actions.
    The Queen of Swords in the past position indicates that
you are a person of ideas, with a good mind. There is a sense
of taking action here, even though the only card which really
indicates that action is the Page of Pentacles (trust your
intuition!).

Pages and Aces tend to deal with new beginnings. The Page of Pentacles in the foundation indicates that you are beginning to move forward and to create new things in your physical world, which may serve to bring about a change of environment, home, or career.

The two focus cards of this reading are the Six and Four of Cups. There's a sense of compassion here, and of sensitivity, which is combined with the six, the number of service. Notice the picture in the Four of Cups, of a hand coming out of the clouds holding the cup, which looks exactly like the Ace of Cups. That symbol, expressing a one, reemphasizes the Ace of Wands, and the quality of new beginnings.

The card at the top of the diamond, representing the Best That Can Come to Pass from the Situation, is the Wheel of Fortune. The Wheel of Fortune can deal with growth, evolution, and karma. This card indicates that you have come to a time where you have an opportunity to move on, and take action on the reason that you came here.

Line of Probability for the future: Ace of Wands. As with any Ace, this card deals with new beginnings. In particular, the Ace of Wands deals with spiritual initiation. As you allow yourself to be open, new spiritual insights will begin coming to you, and you will create a greater capacity for an enlightening spiritual experience. The spiritual energy coming in will bring with it greater opportunity to empower the ideas that you've had in mind for years. Accepting the opportunity with sensitivity, delight, and joy will empower the Page of Pentacles, allowing new things to unfold in your physical environment.

In the Attitudes position is the Three of Cups, which is the card of Joy. It can also be a celebration of the Harvest.

In the Home and Environment position is the High Priestess. This card deals with intuition and receptivity. Numerologically, though, it's a two, which means that it also deals with choices, and duality. This card indicates that you have an opportunity in your life right now, a coming to the fork in the road where you have a choice. Either you can continue on the old path, which has been frustrating for you, or you can move along a new path. The new path is one of independence and self-empowerment, of allowing your higher wisdom and guidance to come through, *and acting on it.* Your environment is going to afford you opportunities to take ideas and make them tangible. It's up to you to follow your intuition and allow that to come to pass.

In the Hopes and Fears Position is the Nine of Swords. In a classical sense, this is the card of worry. However, the overall energy in this pattern is basically positive. The only card that comes up as a hindrance is this Nine of Swords. It seems that basically, the only thing that can hinder you is needless worry. To counter this tendency, maintain balance and proper perspective, remaining alert to the opportunities that come along. Resist trying to figure out too far in advance how things are going to look, and instead make the most of NOW. If you do this, then the future will take care of itself.

Line of Probability for Outcome: Knight of Cups and the Temperance Card. The wings and the silver of the Knight of Cups conveys a sense of intuitive messages, of using sensitivity and intuition to receive guidance. The Temperance card has a strong emphasis on balance. Together, these two cards indicate that you've got an opportunity to bring through the inner wisdom that you have, to use it in balance, and to blend it with the other elements present.

Overall, the pattern that you've already set up is leading you in the direction of the Ace of Wands, the spiritual initiation. The Knight of Cups, with that initiation, is the opportunity for more clear messages to come through and the opportunity to use them in balance—spiritually, mentally, emotionally, and physically. There may have been areas in the past where the mind was active, and the spiritual work done, but because that energy wasn't able to come all the way into physical expression, there were things that may have been unfulfilling emotionally and physically. The Wheel of Fortune card indicates that you have positioned yourself so that you have the opportunity to break old patterns, and to instead empower patterns where your inner wisdom and authority comes through. One of the challenges that you may have this lifetime is to learn how to take nebulous things and bring them down to earth and make them practical. The cards indicate that you are on the verge of making that breakthrough. You'll be able to act upon the inner messages that you receive, and to experience success emotionally, bringing through joy and creating abundance on the physical plane.

Let's take a look at the clarification cards pulled by the reader: Strength, the Five of Cups, King of Wands, and The Moon.

The first card that comes up is the card of Strength, which represents the astrological sign, Leo. Numerologically, eight is the number of strength, and this card indicates that true power comes from inner authority.

The Five of Cups can be a quality of don't cry over spilt milk. This ties in with the fork in the road. Anytime we come to a major choice in life, there will be certain payoffs and certain things that will be left behind. You will have a choice, once you have made the decision, to either focus on the opportunities ahead or to turn around and focus on what you have released. If you focus on what you don't have anymore, then in essence you do a 180-degree loop, and come right back into this same old pattern. If, on the other hand, you can lovingly bless the things that are passing out of your life, and seize the cups that are still upright, you can move forward into a new direction.

The King of Wands represents someone who has achieved a lot of spiritual wisdom and is sharing that wisdom. The kingly quality indicates both mastery and the assertive nature.

Lastly, we have The Moon card, which astrologically represents the sign of Pisces. Pisces is considered to be the most psychic and sensitive of all the signs. The Moon can reflect suppressed garbage or spiritual insight surfacing to conscious awareness. Part of the process for you right now is to take the lid off, and allow things to surface. Some of the things that will surface you might not like. If that happens, look at them, but be as detached as possible. Realize that decisions, choices, and actions of the past were made from the most enlightened perspective that you had at that time. Don't be hard on yourself, don't be hard on others, but experience it, love it, bless it, and release it. And, when things come up from your treasure trove, from the abundance of who you are, then love, bless, and use them.

SEEKER #1, READING #2

This reading presented an opportunity to reword the seeker's question for the proper clarity and focus, from "Tell me about this person" to "Give me advice that can help me in my relationship with this person."

As a special note, while shuffling the cards for this spread, the Two of Swords and the Six of Wands fell out. These cards were replaced, and the entire deck shuffled. The seeker selected the following cards:

Celtic Cross Spread

1 Six of Wands comes back up. (Focus)
2 Two of Swords comes back up.
      (Crossing)
3 King of Swords (Best)
4 The World (21) (Foundation)
5 Ten of Cups (Past)
6 The Lovers (6) (Future)
7 King of Pentacles
      (Attitude)
8 Knight of Cups (Home &
      Environment)
9 Four of Wands (Hopes & Fears)
10 Two of Pentacles (Outcome)
11 Temperance (14)
12 Nine of Swords.
      (Use cards 10, 11, and 12 all in the position of
      card #10, as line of probability for outcome.)

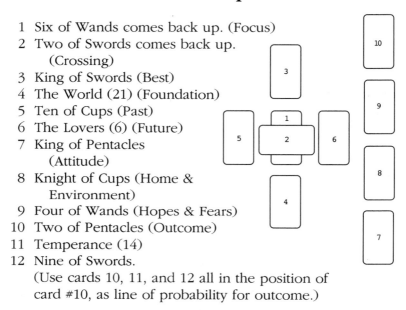

Clarification Cards
* The Tower (16)
* Page of Cups
* Five of Pentacles

      The first impression of this reading is that you are going
through a transition, a transformation, and that if you so
choose, you are coming from a position of power. The first
two cards that came up (also the two cards which fell out) give
you the entire reading. The Six of Wands, which is the victory
card, deals with service. The Two of Swords deals with coming
to a crossroad, and not being sure which way to go. Operate
from strength, and from spiritual guidance, and you will
absolutely know how to respond and act in every situation
that arises.

The World card in the Foundation position gives you unlimited opportunities. The Ten of Cups in the past position is addressing the whole issue of the happy home and family. The card at the top, the King of Swords, is the mate to the Queen of Swords, which has already come up for you. This card deals with acting on the ideas that you receive. Line of Probability for Future is The Lovers. This represents the inner marriage—the marriage made in heaven. You have put yourself into a position where you can operate from strength and from spiritual insight, to make decisions that were perhaps more difficult for you to make in the past, and that lead you in the direction of inner harmony. The King of Pentacles indicates a desire to create more abundance on the physical plane. The Knight of Cups comes up again in the Home and Environment position—a way that you can apply your sensitivity and your psychic ability. Hopes and Fears: The Four of Wands, spiritual success, greater freedom for yourself. Line of Probability for Outcome: Two of Pentacles, the Temperance card, and the Nine of Swords. The Two of Pentacles indicates ups and downs in the material world, which will require you to maintain a balance (Temperance), and to not worry excessively (Nine of Swords).

Here you have a perfect playing out in your relationship of the crossroad that came up in the first spread: you have the choice of empowerment or entrapment. The latter results in needless worry. As you choose to operate from inner power and authority, opportunities arise for you to see clearly what option is best to take. You have set yourself on a course which will bring about the marriage made in heaven—which is within yourself. Not everything is rosy. Issues will arise and you will experience uncertainty and turbulence on the physical plane.

You are the center of your universe, of your relationship. It seems that this relationship provides you with an opportunity to develop your own inner authority, which may mean putting your foot down, and saying: "What I need is this . . ." and either it can be fulfilled within the relationship, or it won't be. But either way, as you take those steps, everything is going to play out naturally. This choice will probably create some turbulence, which will provide you the opportunity and the challenge of staying balanced as it occurs. All of it is going to help you to grow as a person.

The clarification cards selected by the reader were The Tower (need we say more?), Page of Cups, and the Five of Pentacles. The Page of Cups brings with it a quality of a new relationship, although this doesn't necessarily have to be with another person. If this relationship is transformed, energetically, it becomes a new relationship. The Five of Pentacles reminds you that you have a choice of focus—on the stained-glass window, or on the beggars out in the snow. The Tower represents a major breaking up of structure, and the fallout may mirror the choice of focus you made with the Five of Pentacles.

SEEKER #1, READING #3.

Here, the seeker requested information concerning whether or not to accept a job offer. The seeker pulled a few cards to find out what would happen if the job was taken, and a few cards to see what energies would play out if they decided not to take the job.

First, how the energies would play out if the job was taken for the summer.

    Alternative #1:
    1 Ace of Wands
    2 Knight of Swords
    3 Nine of Pentacles
    4 Wheel of Fortune (10)
    * The Star (17) (clarification)

The deck was cut two or three times, to clear out the energies. Then a few cards were pulled to look at how the energies might play out if the seeker decided not to do this work this summer.

Alternative #2:
1 The Hierophant (5)
2 Page of Wands
3 Death (13)
4 Queen of Cups
* The Fool (0) (clarification)

In Alternative #1, the cards chosen were the Ace of Wands, the Knight of Swords, the Nine of Pentacles, and the Wheel of Fortune. The clarification card pulled by the reader was The Star card. Two of these four cards have already come up in the general reading. None of the cards for the second question were in the general reading. This indicates that a pattern has already been set in motion to take the job.

Stepping back from this and looking at the general energy pattern: there is a sense of starting something new with the Ace, but not a strong spiritual sense, just a sense of new beginnings. (Trust your intuition, even when the sense you get of the card shifts its usual meaning.) With the Knight of Swords, there is a sense of inner conflict—wanting to do it, and not wanting to do it. But the payoff is the Nine of Pentacles, of feeling freer financially. The Wheel of Fortune carries a sense of fulfilling an obligation. With The Star, the word that comes up is freedom.

Looking at Alternative #2, which concerns the energy if the job isn't taken, you have The Hierophant—the spiritual calling, a quality of God-Within, and like the Page of Wands, a person treading on a new path. It is a five, which is a number of freedom. So this choice would deal with creating greater freedom. Then there is the Page of Wands, which represents the person who is treading on a new path, so there is a quality of newness and openness. The Death card represents major change. The Queen of Cups deals with receptivity, and The Fool deals with walking in faith. There are no swords or pentacles. Lofty ideas are dealt with here, but there's nothing tangible, nothing physical.

With the first layout, you don't have the emotional payoff, because there are no Cups, but you do have the Major Arcana, the Wands, the Swords, and the Pentacles. And the pentacle which comes up is the Nine of Pentacles, which is a card of completion, of something being completed on the physical plane. You also have The Wheel of Fortune, which is a card of karmic obligation and karmic freedom. Choice No. 1 is a more grounded choice. Choice No. 2 reaches up more into the higher spheres, but it doesn't bring anything into the physical plane. The more practical approach takes care of the financial needs. Additionally, The Star card in Alternative #1 can be viewed as leading to an opportunity for something down the road. The Star is a seventeen, which reduces to an eight, which is a power number. This is the first eight which has come up in any of the readings and may indicate that some aspect of empowering yourself is tied into taking this job.

Alternative #2 is based upon wanting to have freedom, with The Hierophant, and wanting to walk the spiritual path, making major changes, following that intuition and being sensitive, but yet there's nothing that grounds any of this. On first blush, the energy pattern of the second alternative seemed great, but then upon tuning in, there wasn't anything there, like a balloon with no string. The Fool says it all. The Fool can be the person who is so walking in the light of God, that everything falls into place. But when not used in balance, it represents the person who makes foolish decisions. So we come back to the crux: in everything there is a time and a season.

Readings for Seeker #2

SEEKER #2, READING #1

This is a birthday reading. The birthday begins the first period in the new solar cycle, which lasts one year. Thus a birthday reading can give a very clear picture of the energy and patterns already being projected. The first phase is also the best period for initiating new patterns that will be in play for the rest of the year.

For good information on the seven phases of the solar cycle, see *Wisdom of the Mystic Masters,* by Joseph Weed.

We will begin with a general reading to cover the year. The seeker drew 11 cards, with 3 clarification cards pulled by the reader.

Celtic Cross Spread

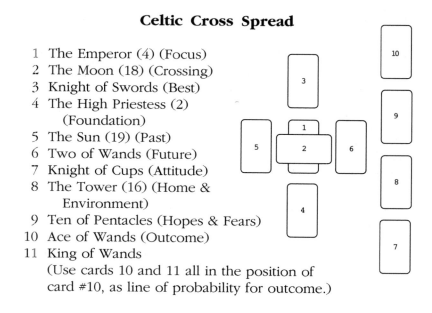

1 The Emperor (4) (Focus)
2 The Moon (18) (Crossing)
3 Knight of Swords (Best)
4 The High Priestess (2)
    (Foundation)
5 The Sun (19) (Past)
6 Two of Wands (Future)
7 Knight of Cups (Attitude)
8 The Tower (16) (Home &
    Environment)
9 Ten of Pentacles (Hopes & Fears)
10 Ace of Wands (Outcome)
11 King of Wands
    (Use cards 10 and 11 all in the position of
    card #10, as line of probability for outcome.)

Clarification Cards
* Eight of Wands
* Justice (11)
* Page of Pentacles

The initial impression of this spread is of being at a point of great opportunity. Five of the eleven cards are Major Arcana cards. This indicates that there is a lot of energy present to work with, and that opportunities for transformation abound. Overall, this energy is positive and balanced.

The first two cards are often the core of the reading. Both of these cards are Major Arcana cards, which indicates that there are some fairly intense things going on. The first card is The Emperor, and the second is The Moon.

The Emperor is a four, the number of structure. Here you have a man sitting on a throne made of concrete—that's about as solid as you can get! This is a good focus card, with a spiritual quality about it.

The crossing card, The Moon, represents Pisces. This card shows a lobster coming out of the water, symbolic of things surfacing. Together, these cards indicate that a good foundation has been laid, and that it is now time for additional insights or fears to surface into the light of understanding.

The High Priestess in the Foundation position deals with insight, intuition, and reflection. It looks like a foundation issue for the next year will be allowing more intuition and receptivity to surface. This may mean allowing opportunities to come to you.

The Sun Card is in the Past position. This card has a quality of living life like a little child, really enjoying things, and just taking things one step at a time.

The card which is in the position of the Best That Can Come to Pass from the Situation is the Knight of Swords. There is a sense here of "go for it." Trust the process, trust yourself. Even so, there may be some apprehension. It looks like this horse has a little bit of fear in his eyes. There may be times when you will doubt where you are going; then it is important to act upon faith and intuition, without necessarily having anything concrete to back it up. Feel the fear and do it anyway.

In the Line of Probability for Future position is the Two of Wands. This card shows a man holding the world in his hand. This represents that you have choices, and that with those choices comes virtually unlimited potential.

In the Attitudes Position is the Knight of Cups. The wings on the helmet, like Hermes, represents communication. The color silver represents working with the nature of the Moon— the receptive, sensitive, or intuitive nature. This card is an affirmation of where your attention is.

In the position of Home and Environment is The Tower card. This card would be a concern if other cards in this spread indicated disharmony or discord. However, all the other cards have a very positive energy indicating some structures may be broken. It's interesting: the first card is The Emperor, talking about a structure that has been formed, and yet this new energy coming in indicates some of that structure is going to be broken up. It is quite possible there may be some very rapid transformation in how you see yourself, the work that you do, possibly even where you live, or the places you travel to. With those changes come opportunity, and with opportunities come the potentials for growth.

In the Hopes and Fears position is the Ten of Pentacles. This card seems to mirror the energy of the Two of Wands. The Wands deal with spiritual nature, and the Pentacles deal with physical nature. As above, so below. Not only is there spiritual abundance, as indicated by the Two of Wands, but also the potential of physical abundance, as indicated by the Ten of Pentacles.

In the Line of Probability for Outcome position, there is the Ace of Wands and the King of Wands. Aces usually deal with new beginnings, Wands with spirituality. This could indicate that you are moving in the direction of a spiritual initiation that could really shake up things in the next year, coming as it does after The Tower card. The King of Wands would be the person who utilizes those transformative insights, perhaps in their work as a teacher.

Overall, this is a very nice spread, a very nice reading, and it indicates that you are on the right track. There is an emphasis on your spiritual energy and the importance of staying spiritually connected, especially considering the radical changes which may take place in your life.

The three clarification cards are an affirmation of what's come up in the Celtic Cross spread. There's the Eight of Wands, the Justice card, and the Page of Pentacles. Eight is a power number, and Wands deal with spirit, so the Eight of Wands is indicating spiritual power being brought into alignment. These wands are not *perfectly* aligned, but they are moving in the right direction. The Justice card numerologically is an eleven, which is the number of the spiritual light messenger. Additionally, this card has a quality of maintaining balance. The Page of Pentacles refers to a person who may have a new project or projects coming out. Who knows what may come about in the next three hundred and sixty-five days? There are a lot of opportunities on the horizon, and even more will come up that you are not aware of at this point.

SEEKER #2, READING #2

This is a time line pyramid for the coming year. The seeker has selected eleven cards.

1 Seven of Swords (Eight of Pentacles to clarify)
2 Three of Swords (Ten of Cups to clarify)
3 The World (21)
4 Three of Cups
5 Death (13)
6 Six of Swords

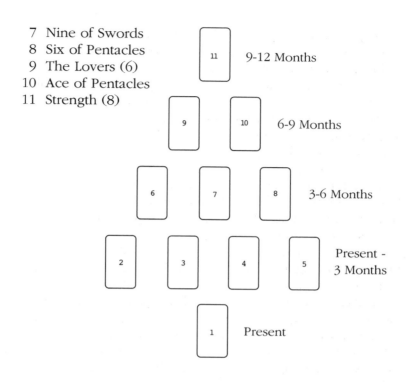

7 Nine of Swords
8 Six of Pentacles
9 The Lovers (6)
10 Ace of Pentacles
11 Strength (8)

11   9-12 Months

9   10   6-9 Months

6   7   8   3-6 Months

2   3   4   5   Present -
                        3 Months

1   Present

The first card, dealing with the present, is the Seven of Swords. Numerologically, the seven represents spirituality. Swords tend to deal with the mental plane. This card shows a man very diligently placing some swords in line. On one hand, this can be a card of putting your house in order and making sure that everything is okay. But this can also be the theft card, the thief in the night. To get greater clarity on this, another card was selected, the Eight of Pentacles. This card has a very positive upbeat energy, possibly representing a person who has a lot of talents, or who is making money. Numerologically, eight is a power number. This energy indicates that the Seven of Swords should be viewed in a positive way, as indicating that you are spiritually and mentally putting things into alignment. The Eight of Pentacles may indicate that, as a result, you will see some of the fruits of this process in the material plane.

Going up to the next level, dealing with the next three months, there's the Three of Swords, The World card, the Three of Cups, and the Death card. Interestingly, numerologically we have three threes. There is a real emphasis here upon creative self-expression. The Death card deals with major transformation. In the next three months it looks as if there is going to be a transformation in the way you express your creativity. The Three of Swords can be a really sad situation, one which results in heartache. The World card can represent unlimited opportunities, with ending a cycle and beginning a new cycle. The Three of Cups can deal with celebrating a harvest.

A clarification card was selected to give some guidance as to how to work positively with the energy of the Three of Swords. The card pulled was the Ten of Cups, the card of the happy home and family. So, something may come up regarding a relationship, one which initially looks very sad, but out of which something very good can come.

On the next level is the Six of Swords, the Nine of Swords, and the Six of Pentacles. Again, you have another numerological pattern, with two sixes. At this point, there's a focus upon service and finding truth. The Nine of Swords can be worry, the Six of Swords can be travel. The Six of Pentacles can be a card of service through sharing of one's time, talent, and/or treasure. In this three-month period you may have the opportunity to travel and to be of service, but tend to worry over things like scheduling.

We're now going up to the next level, the level dealing with the time period of six months to nine months. On this level are The Lovers and the Ace of Pentacles. Aces usually deal with new beginnings, and Pentacles deal with the physical plane. What I see here is the possibility of new money coming in, perhaps from business ventures previously invested in. The Lovers card can signify the joy that comes from those material blessings, but more so than that, I view it as representing the inner lover, or inner harmony. It can also represent a love relationship. The Lovers is another six, so it looks as if the theme of service continues. It may be that, through service having been provided in the past and currently being provided, monetary benefits will come to you, as well as the possibility of inner joy, serenity, happiness, and yes, a possible love relationship.

Now we go to the top of the time line pyramid. This deals with the period of nine months to twelve months. The last card is The Strength card. Numerologically, this is an eight, which is the power number. This card seems to symbolize, above all others, inner strength. So there is a good matching between The Lovers card of the previous period and the Strength card of this period. Having just experienced contentment and inner harmony leads naturally to even greater levels of inner strength, as signified by the Strength card.

The energy of the last two periods seems to lead naturally to the conclusion that major projects and goals will likely come to a successful resolution. This success will build inner confidence and strength which can be utilized to launch a new set of projects and goals.

SEEKER #2, READING #3

In view of the scope of the last two readings, the seeker would like to ask three questions: what does he have to teach, what can be learned now, and what to focus on for the coming year.

Question #1:
1 The Hierophant (5)
2 Temperance (14)

Question #2:
1 Four of Pentacles

Question #3:
1 Four of Wands
2 King of Cups

First: for the coming year, what does the seeker have to teach? The seeker pulled two cards (actually only one, and the other one popped out with it): The Hierophant and Temperance. The Hierophant represents a quality of God-Within, and numerologically, it is a five.

The other card that has come up is the Temperance card, which emphasizes balance. It is a fourteen, which reduces to a five. Numerologically, fives can deal with freedom, change, and flexibility. Along with recognizing that God is found within, it looks like freedom, change, and flexibility are going to be the qualities you teach this year. Bear in mind the maxim: We best teach what we most need to learn.

Next: What lesson can be learned now? Here, the seeker selected the Four of Pentacles. This card shows a fellow holding one of the pentacles very tightly, as if concerned about loss. This seems to say, don't get too wrapped up in financial concerns, or concerns about the physical. This year it looks like you will learn to allow for the ebb and flow. And as part of this process, be aware that some things may be released, thus creating an opportunity for something else to come in.

Lastly: What should they focus on for the coming year? The seeker drew the Four of Wands and the King of Cups. This Four of Wands is very much a pastoral card, of time spent in nature to relax. Additionally, there's a feeling of celebration. It seems your focus should be on relaxing and holding a joyous spiritual nature. Then the King of Cups would be the individual who is willing to share that.

As an interesting note, none of the cards drawn by seeker #2 were repeated in any of the other spreads. Perhaps for this individual, variety is the spice of life.

15

CONCLUSION

Our journey through the Tarot has come to an end. However, as with all things in life, an ending is merely a new beginning, and the Tarot, in its richness and fullness, is a lifelong study, ever unfolding. We see this with the never-ending cycle represented in the Major Arcana cards. Upon completing a project, The World, one immediately moves into The Fool, experiencing the abyss, the unknown. However, in this space is tremendous power, for here, all things are possible, all directions are open. A wise person becomes still, contacting their God-Self, and receives guidance for their perfect new beginning. The choices you make set your feet upon a new path, a new adventure. Your focus invokes The Magician energy, empowers your new course, and so a new cycle is birthed.

As you reflect upon where you go from here, realize that the material in this book, without application, is worthless. It is only theory and "head stuff." However, through testing the principles, experimenting with the exercises, and practice, practice, practice, you will find what works for you. Application will result in concepts becoming inner knowing and wisdom. When this is coupled with regular meditation and quiet time, spiritual revelations *will* occur.

We have touched upon many areas, including spiritual and metaphysical principles, meditation and other forms of inner attunement, numerology, colorology, astrology, and even a little sacred symbology and geometry (this last one was slipped in rather quietly). Knowledge in these areas can be very helpful in advanced Tarot. For further study in these and other subjects, you will find that the bibliography contains some wonderful books.

Our last comment is personal. We believe that every man, woman, and child on this planet has a spark of God within them and a purpose for being here. Working with the Tarot, in conjunction with spiritual practices, has helped us experience a closer connection with God, a greater sense of purpose, and a deeper love for our fellow human beings. As you experience God's love and share it with others, it becomes easier for them to do the same. If this book has assisted you on your spiritual path, then part of our purpose has been fulfilled and we are happy.

BIBLIOGRAPHY AND
SUGGESTED READING

Bach, Richard. (1977). *Illusions: The Adventures of a Reluctant Messiah.* New York: Dell.

Campbell, Florence. (1931, 1958). *Your Days Are Numbered: A Manual of Numerology For Everybody.* The Gateway.

Gawain, Shakti. (1978). *Creative Visualization.* New York: Bantam Books.

Hill, Napoleon. (1972). *Think and Grow Rich.* New York: Hawthorn/Dutton.

Jeanne. (1987). *Numerology: Spiritual Light Vibrations.* Your Center For Truth Press.

Lamsa, George M. (Transl.). (1933). *Holy Bible from the Ancient Eastern Text.* San Francisco: Harper & Row.

Reader's Digest. (1989). Pleasantville, NY: Reader's Digest Association.

Roman, Sanaya. (1986). *Living With Joy.* Tiburon, CA: H. J. Kramer Inc.

Roman, Sanaya. (1986). *Personal Power Through Awareness.* Tiburon, CA: H. J. Kramer Inc.

Roman, Sanaya. (1987). *Opening to Channel.* Tiburon, CA: H. J. Kramer Inc.

Roman, Sanaya. (1989). *Spiritual Growth.* Tiburon, CA: H. J. Kramer Inc.

Roman, Sanaya & Packer, Duane. (1988). *Creating Money: Keys to Abundance.* Tiburon, CA: H. J. Kramer Inc.

Smith, Stretton. (1993). *4-T Prosperity Program.* Carmel, CA: 4-T Publishing Co.

Szekely, Edmond B. (1976). *The Gospel of the Essenes.* Great Britain: Hillman Printers (Frome) Ltd.

Weed, Joseph. (1968). *Wisdom of the Mystic Masters.* Parker Publishing Co.

Zerner, Amy & Farber, Monte. (1990). *The Enchanted Tarot.* New York: St. Martin's Press.

RICHARD GORDON

Since becoming a spiritual/metaphysical teacher in 1980, Richard Gordon has taught in about eighty different centers in the United States, Europe, and South America. His teaching and counseling focus on such subjects as meditation, inner attunement, relaxation, creative visualization, universal principles, Tarot, numerology, and astrology. His purpose is to promote spiritual enlightenment, personal empowerment, and positive planetary transformation.

Richard produces and distributes internationally a series of audio and video cassettes. His video *How to Read the Tarot Cards: A Metaphysical Approach* has been a best-seller in the United States since 1987. Additional videos include *How to Pray and Meditate* and *Crystal Contemplation.* His guided meditation audio cassettes are entitled *Journey to the Golden Pyramid* and *Spiritual Light Journey.* The former was a 1993 finalist for the Golden Headset Award in the best inspirational self-help category. As a result of the interest generated by the Tarot video, Richard has written his first book, *The Intuitive Tarot.* This work, published in Spring 1994, combines material from the popular Tarot video with previously unreleased information.

With a Bachelor of Science degree in Chemical Engineering and several years' experience in the petroleum industry, Richard approaches the area of metaphysics from a scientific base. In 1980, he became Director of the Baton Rouge School of Metaphysics, leaving in 1981 to begin a self-development program which included completion of the Self-Realization

Fellowship lessons, an initiation into Kriya Yoga, and EST Training. He served on the Board of Directors of the Louisiana Society for Personal Realization in 1978–88 and 1990–91 and was its president from 1991–92.

Richard's abilities have taken a new but inevitable turn. It is quite natural that his interest in light, color, sound, and transformation should turn to motion pictures. In 1993, he became a pivotal force in joining producer/director Howard Kipp Parker's production group in the development of the action-adventure motion picture, *The Psychenaut*.

Richard continues to give workshops and seminars throughout the country. You may contact Richard Gordon, 10147 Jefferson Highway, Baton Rouge, LA 70809.

DIXIE TAYLOR

Poet, singer, songwriter, actress and artist, Dixie Taylor is the wordsmith behind *The Intuitive Tarot*. Dixie extracted the material from Richard's Tarot video and audio tapes and, after editing, reorganizing, and processing, added her voice and insights to the work. Her ability to weave word magic has brought these concepts to life with love and wisdom.

Dixie is a collection of soul qualities with multi-faceted expressions. A poet by nature and lawyer by training, Dixie brings simplicity to logical thought, and grounded balancing to intuitive knowlege. She writes in a variety of genres, including poetry, short stories, children's stories and plays; sings, writes and performs music on the guitar with her group, "My, My, My!"; sculpts masks and fairies; and dabbles in other visual medias. Simplicity, joy, and laughter are the gifts she brings to the path of clarity and wisdom. Curiosity is the gift she brings to life.

You may contact Dixie Taylor, P.O. Box 15086, Baton Rouge, LA 70895.

Richard Gordon's Video Cassettes

This video has been on New Leaf's Best-seller List since 1988.

How to Read the Tarot Cards

This 90-minute tape shows why video is the perfect how-to medium. Richard Gordon takes the viewer through a card reading, step-by-step, in a presentation that is easy to follow and yet encourages the development of your own intuition. An excellent video to complement the book—for experienced readers wanting to enhance their skills as well as beginners delving into Tarot for the first time.

90-minute video VHS
ISBN: 0-931892-85-6 $39.95

Crystal Contemplation

Crystal Contemplation is a relaxing and inspiring half-hour of visual imagery and musical expression. Moving crystal images, gentle lighting changes, harmonious harp, and relaxing voice are combined to paint a unique mosaic. Stress, tension, and anxiety melt away as they are replaced by peace and harmony.

30-minute video VHS
ISBN: 0-931892-89-9 $27.85

Richard Gordon's Audio Cassettes

60-minute audio, $10
ISBN: 0-931892-82-1

Spiritual Light Journey

Discover the universe within and enjoy the complete freedom from stress and worry with *Spiritual Light Journey*. Richard created this guided meditation tape "for personal transformation and planetary healing." An exceptional feature is an extended interlude of original music by Craig Evans. This tape is only listening distance away from your inner world of healing beauty and truth.

Journey to the Golden Pyramid

One of ten nominees for a national best-spoken audio award for 1993, this guided meditation can be used to relieve the day's pressure and allow you to journey back into yourself. The enchanting blend of Richard's voice and the harp music of Gail Barber gently guide you to your personal sanctuary of peace, love, and wisdom within.
60-minute audio, $10.

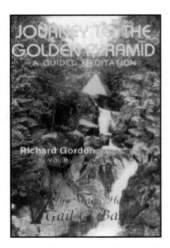

ISBN: 0-931892-83-X

Order from Blue Dolphin Publishing, Inc. • 1-800-643-0765
or use order form at back of book.

Books from
Blue Dolphin Publishing

Your Mind Knows More Than You Do
The Subconscious Secrets of Success
Sidney Friedman
ISBN: 1-57733-052-8, 184 pp., $22.00, hardcover
over 10,000 copies sold

Becoming the Husband Your Wife Thought She Married
It's Your Life, Too, Man
James A. Schaller, M.D.
ISBN: 1-57733-059-5, 308 pp., $16.95

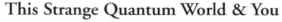

Starch Madness
Paleolithic Nutrition for Today
Richard L. Heinrich
ISBN: 1-57733-027-7, 176 pp., $12.95
The best "diet" book for today

This Strange Quantum World & You
Patricia Topp
ISBN: 1-57733-035-8, 64 pp., $8.95
Physics for 9 – 90

Invocations to the Light
Wistancia Stone
ISBN: 1-57733-011-0, 176 pp., $12.95
With invocations, we become magnets . . .

Books from
Blue Dolphin Publishing

Stepparenting Without Guilt
Maurine Doerken
ISBN: 1-57733-054-4, 152 pp., $11.00

Journal of Love
Spiritual Communication with Animals Through Journal Writing
Jan Kolb
ISBN: 1-57733-046-3, 184 pp., $14.95

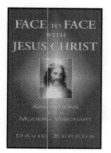

Face to Face with Jesus Christ
Apparitions to a Modern Visionary
David Sereda
ISBN: 1-57733-032-3, 278pp., $14.95

I, Joseph of Arimathea
A Story of Jesus, His Resurrection, and the Aftermath: A Documented Historical Novel
Frank C. Tribbe
ISBN: 1-57733-061-7, 412 pp., $19.95

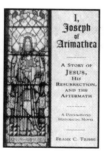

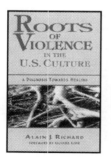

Roots of Violence in the U.S. Culture
A Diagnosis Toward Healing
Alain Richard
ISBN: 1-57733-043-9, 160 pp., $14.95

People of the Circle, People of the Four Directions
Scott McCarthy
ISBN: 1-57733-013-7, 712 pp., $34.95

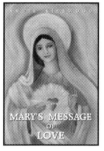

Books from
Blue Dolphin Publishing

Mary's Message of Love
As Sent by Mary, the Mother of Jesus, to Her Messenger
Annie Kirkwood
ISBN: 0-931892-33-3, 152 pp., $14.95, new second edition

A Guide to the Dolphin Divination Cards
102 Oracular Readings Inspired by the Dolphins
Nancy Clemens
ISBN: 1-57733-017-X, 380 pp., $18.00

Dolphin Divination Cards
Nancy Clemens
ISBN: 0-931892-79-1, 108 circular cards, $11.00, boxed
over 30,000 copies sold

Aura Awareness
What Your Aura Says About You
C.E. Lindgren & Jennifer Baltz, Eds.
ISBN: 0-9652490-5-0, 160 pp., 8 pp. color, $12.95

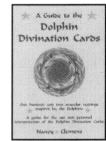

Capturing the Aura
Integrating Science, Technology, and Metaphysics
C.E. Lindgren, Ed.
ISBN: 1-57733-072-2, 368 pp., $19.95